I0094497

PARTY LIST SYSTEM:
ITS ADVOCACIES, FUNCTIONS, AND PROGRAM INVOLVEMENT

Philippine Research Colloquium Volume 11

ALEXIS V. BELARMINO
ANGELITO Y. AVILES
JHON VINCENT M. AVELINO
MARVIN M. MAGTABOG
NEIL ADRIAN C. PASTRANA

PARTY LIST SYSTEM:
ITS ADVOCACIES, FUNCTIONS, AND PROGRAM INVOLVEMENT

Philippine Research Colloquium Volume 11

GALDA VERLAG 2018

Bibliografische Information der Deutschen Nationalbibliothek
Die Deutsche Nationalbibliothek verzeichnet diese Publikation in der Deutschen
Nationalbibliografie; detaillierte bibliografische Daten sind im Internet über
http://dnb.ddb.de abrufbar.

© 2018 Galda Verlag, Glienicke
Neither this book nor any part may be reproduced or transmitted in any form or by any means
electronic or mechanical, including photocopying, micro-filming, and recording, or by any
information storage or retrieval system, without prior permission in writing from the publisher.
Direct all inquiries to Galda Verlag, Franz-Schubert-Str. 61, 16548 Glienicke, Germany

ISBN 978-3-96203-051-3 (Print)
ISBN 978-3-96203-052-0 (E-Book)

Originally presented as the authors thesis at
Rizal Technological University - College of Arts and Sciences, Manila 2018

ACKNOWLEDGEMENTS

The researchers' great appreciation goes to the several individuals whom in the one way or another have made this research possible. Without their contributions in small or large measure, they could have not finished this study.

They convey their utmost gratitude and sincerest appreciation to the following person concerted their time and efforts.

Prof. Rafael Y. Paragas, Prof. Apple Kate S. Sabar and Prof. Nouvie N. Aguirre, who had given so much efforts in giving, sharing their knowledge, and validating the thesis interview questionnaire. They also provided improvement on the instrument of the study.

Honorable Representatives from Bayan Muna, Akbayan, CIBAC, KABAYAN, ACT Teachers and Magdalo Party list, for patiently and honestly answering the interview questionnaires provided by the researchers.

Rizal Technological University CAS Library, for the books and computer resources that they used for doing the study, for letting the researchers to stay in the library premises from the beginning and upon the completion of the study.

Dr. Virginia S. Sobremisana, the researchers' thesis professor, for her never ending support and guidance throughout the whole research. Also, for her willingness and dedication to help the researchers until the study has been completed.

Prof. Michael M. Mesinas, the researchers' thesis adviser, for his outstanding effort of encouragement, support and patience in editing and correcting the research study. Also, for sharing his knowledge as well as guiding the researchers all throughout this study with words of enthusiasm.

To the Researchers' Family, who gave moral and financial support to pursue this study and also for their undying love, support and guidance and provided such strength and inspirational words to the researchers.

And of course, to Almighty God, who bestowed the clarity of the heart and mind to finish this study and making all things possible, thus glory and praise, be given unto him.

A.V.B A.Y.A

JV.M.A

M.M.M NA.C.P

ABSTRACT

The main purpose of this study is to determine the advocacies, functions and program involvement of the Party list System in the Congress in relation to the marginalized/unprivileged sectors of the society. A total of 6 respondents were selected from Party list groups at House of Representatives, Quezon City. The researchers used qualitative research design to gather in-depth understanding about Party List System in the Philippines.

Through the establishment and creation of Republic Act No. 7941 or "Party list System Act of 1995", marginalized/unprivileged sectors have now the chance to be represented in the Congress with the initiative of the Party list Representatives. These representatives serve as the face, voice and representation of those in the different sectors of the society. It helps them through their advocacies, functions and program involvement such as the bills/ laws they filed in the Congress.

The researchers would like to recommend to all the concerned individuals that, in order to achieve total transparency, equality and rightful representation in the Congress, each one should learn how to value everyone's worth, live with accordance of the law and appreciate diversity. Moreover, everybody should share the positivity to everyone by lending hands to those who are in need most especially in the marginalized/unprivileged sectors of the society. Also, we should believe to their skills and capabilities about what they could do to lift their economic status away from poverty, corruption and discrimination. Thus, the researchers entrusted the protection and promotion of general welfare to the Party List Representatives by proposing or legislating appropriate laws/bills in connection to the fast development and proper representation of the marginalized/unprivileged sectors in the Congress.

TABLE OF CONTENTS

21 METHODOLOGY

24 RESULTS AND DISCUSSION

54 APPENDICES

1

THE PROBLEM AND ITS BACKGROUND

Introduction

The Philippines is a democratic and republican state. Sovereignty resides in its people and all government authority emanates from them (1987 Philippine Constitution).

Such striking provision brought by the Constitution, it gives forth to a new spirit in which every Filipino partakes, shares and holds in the authority exercised by our government. Unfortunately, it is pity that a Filipino suffers because of instability in politics and the government's inadequacy to govern its people.

Politics, according to Oxford Dictionary, are the activities associated with the governance of a country or other area, especially the debate or conflict among individuals or parties having or hoping to achieve power. The activities of government concerning the political relations between countries and within an organization which aimed to improve someone's status or position are typically considered to be devious as the assumption and principles relating to or inherent in a sphere, theory or things, especially when concerned with power and status in a society.

However, Philippine politics is largely controlled by the economic elites. Electoral competition does not revolve around class differences. Instead, it is a game played within the elite classes who manipulates and controls the whole political process including election participation of the people. In fact, there is no substantial people's participation from the masses in decision-making and governance. But as time goes by, Philippines is now fortunate with a good system of government, which will always look to the current situation of its people and will always be there to hear their thoughts. Nowadays, Filipinos can actively participate and select those who they think can help them propose and formulate proper laws, bills and policies.

Moreover, in an attempt of the government to continue providing a better life for its people, the government adopted the Party list System which was already common in European countries. Filipino legislators innovates the Party list System in the Philippines and it was introduced in the Constitution to empower the voice and political participation of the people. Also, in compliance with its constitutional duty, Congress passed the Republic Act No. 7941 also known as "Party list System Act of 1995" as the enabling law of the Party list members in the country.

The Party list System primarily seeks to ensure the equal participation of marginalized and/or underrepresented groups or sectors in law-making/ legislative process. As stipulated in its Declaration of Policy, the Party list System will enable Filipino citizens belonging to marginalized and underrepresented sectors, organizations and parties, and who lack well-defined political constituencies but who could contribute to the formulation and enactment of appropriate legislation that will benefit the nation as a whole, to become members of the House of Representatives (Sec. 2, Republic Act No.7941).

Party List Political Representation is used to be understood in terms of a technical device for decision-making processes in groups that cannot possibly meet face to face and which therefore require a form of delegation between clearly defined persons or groups. This representation serves as a medium of all Filipinos to voice out their opinions on contemporary issues. Through this system, a portal of equality and fair treatment in our society opens. It embodies the promise of further democratization by giving an opportunity to various sectors to have their voices be heard.

In addition above, this Political Representation is the activity of making the citizen's voices, opinions and perspectives present in the public policy making processes. This describes how elected officials nominally speak for their constituents and open the ways for democratic citizens to be legitimately represented within a democratic regime (Hanna Pitkin, 1967). Furthermore, a state with a political representation features a government where every voice is heard in the legislative process. Meaning, it provides a clearer perspective for the law makers; from the role of the representatives and constituents, the nature of their relationships, up to the legislative decision making. In this system of representation, the state is built with a solid foundation strengthened by the participation of both constituents and government (Banuegua, 2010).

In this study, the researchers asserted that the problem lies on the advocacies, functions and program involvement of Party list System. That is why, this paper primarily aimed to trace the way the Party List Groups demonstrates their advocacies through the bills they filed, their functions and program involvement and the corresponding actions of their respective representatives in the Congress.

This study proceeded with the cases of six selected multi-sectoral and marginalized parties such as Akbayan, Bayan Muna, CIBAC, KABAYAN, ACT Teachers and Magdalo. From these cases, researchers found out the advocacies, functions and program involvement of the selected Party List groups. The researchers also aimed to demonstrate the real essence of Party List System in the country so that it transforms a well-intended mechanism into something that actually works and benefits the Filipino people.

Theoretical Framework

This study provided a general understanding about the Party-List System using political representation theory that strengthened and gave meaning to the research work on hand.

This study used the theory of Substantive Representation by Hanna Pitkin which cited in dissertation "Discussing Substantive Representation" of Barasa (2011). Substantive Representation theory discussed the tendency of elected legislators to advocate or take action on behalf of the interest of certain groups and be the substitute for the people's beliefs, thoughts and principles in the legislative process.

Therefore, substantive representation theory assessed a representative by the extent to which policy outcomes advanced by said representative serve the best interests of their constituents that no one among the people will be left-out.

INPUT

- Party list System: It's Advocacies, Functions, and Program Involvement

PROCESS

- In-depth interview and Focused group discussion using Interview Sheet Questionnaires.

OUTPUT

- Challenges encountered by the Party-list in the execution of its advocacies, functions and program involvement.

Figure 1: Research Paradigm

The research paradigm of this study discusses the advocacies, functions and program involvement of the Party List System in the Philippines. It used in-depth interview and focused-group using interview sheet questionnaires in data gathering to be able to know the challenges encountered by the Party list in the country.

Statement of the Problem

This study was designed for three purposes: to find out the advocacies, functions and program involvement of Party List System.

Specifically, it attempted to answer the following questions:

1. What is the Political representation of the Party list System
2. What are the advocacies, functions and programs of the selected Party List System?
3. How does Party List prepare, plan and analyze? Do they consult their benefactors?
4. What are the challenges encountered by the Party List Representatives in the course of the delivery of their advocacies, functions and involvement

Significance of the Study

This study finds its significance in the contribution that it might add towards the development of our understanding about the activities involvement of the researchers' chosen parties. Moreover, these humble pieces of work wished to contribute to sectors or fields such as:

Party List Representatives. They may be reminded about the power vested and imparted to them by the Constitution as good public officers and must be paid them with equal public trust.

Respective Sectors. Represented by the Party lists so that they will be reminded that they are not alone in fighting for what they believe and it's now the time that their voices will be heard throughout the country.

Future Political Science Researchers. They may be guided in conceptualizing their work and have some ideas on how their study will flow. Also, may this paper be a source of information in the development of their work for them to have a good outcome study.

People of this Nation. Through this paper, may they learn that they must not only elect or participate just to practice their right of suffrage during local and national elections, but also to educate them on how to evaluate and find good leaders that will lift our nation out from scarcity.

Scope and Delimitation

This study covered the advocacies, functions and program involvement of Party List groups in the Philippines.

The researchers conducted an interview to the six selected multi-sectoral and marginalized Party list members in the Congress namely **Akbayan**, Bayan Muna, CIBAC, KABAYAN, ACT Teachers and Magdalo through their respective offices. They were asked about their advocacies, functions and program involvement inside and outside their offices. Also, they were asked about the status of the current bill they proposed and how effective it were be for their constituents. The researchers will gather data through focused group discussion, in-depth interview and distributed interview sheet questionnaires.

Definition of Terms

For better understanding of the study the following terms are operationally defined:

Alliance of Concerned Teachers (ACT Teachers) Party List – It is a progressive, militant and nationalist organization of teachers, academic non-teaching personnel and non-academic non-teaching personnel. It is also the largest non-traditional teachers' organization in the country which works for the economic and political well-being of teachers and all other education workers.

Advocacy – This is an activity by an individual or group which aims to influence decisions within political, economic, and social systems and institutions. Advocacy can include many activities that a person or organization undertakes including media campaigns, public speaking, commissioning and publishing research or conducting exit poll or the filling of an amicus brief.

Akbayan Citizens' Action Party List – It is a democratic socialist political party in the Philippines. Its primary ideology is participatory democracy and participatory socialism.

Bayan Muna Party – It is a national political party committed to the politics of people empowerment and social change. It is also active in the parliament of the streets engaging in direct actions on a variety of people's issues and concerns.   Bill. Refers to proposed legislation under consideration by a legislature. A bill does not become law until it is passed by the legislature and, in most cases, approved by the executive. Once a bill has been enacted into law, it is called an act or a statute.

Citizens' Battle Against Corruption (CIBAC) Party List – It is a political organization in the Philippines, founded in 1997. It is also dedicated towards fighting graft, corruption and cronyism in government.

Functions – Refer to the activity or purpose natural to or intended for a person or a thing.

Government – Refers to the system by which a state or community is controlled. In the case of this broad associative definition, government normally consists of legislators, administrators, and arbitrators.

Kabalikat Ng Mamamayan (KABAYAN) Party List – It is a ComElec-accredited Party List that represents marginalized sectors of the Filipino community, including the disabled, senior citizens, Overseas Filipino Workers (OFWs), fishermen, farmers, the poor.

Magdalo Para Sa Pilipino Party List – It is a political party in the Philippines. Magdalo represents the retired personnel of the Armed Forces of the Philippines (AFP) and their families, as well as the urban poor and the youth.

Marginalized Sector – Refers to the self-employed or those working in family workshops, jeepney drivers, rural workers like fisher folks and farmers. The nature and operation of their work are beyond the scope and reach of government legislation and regulations on labor as there are no employer-employee relationships.

Party List – Refers to any system of proportional representation in which voters choose among parties rather than among candidates. Party List Representatives. They are those who were chosen or elected by the members of a Party to represent particular groups/sectors in legislative process.

Programs – These are the planned series of future events, items, or performances.

Republic Acts – These are the pieces of legislation used to create policy in order to carry out the principles of the Constitution.

2

REVIEW OF RELATED
LITERATURE

This chapter discusses about the views, related concepts and studies that made a significant contribution in the development of this research.

Party List System: History and Definition

It was found out that both New Zealand and the United States are the ones who conceptualized and incorporated the structural forms of the electoral system but before it was called Party-list, it was once known and derived from the concept of Proportional Representation (PR) electoral system in certain European countries. PR was based on the proportion of votes obtained by a candidate with respect to the totality of votes that will be casted in a specific state and make it possible for minority groups to choose and elect representatives of their choice in single-member districts. It was used as a remedy to cure the basic flaws or disadvantages of the majoritarian or plurality system in their country.

In the United States, this was achieved by drawing special majority- minority districts that maximize the number of blacks in a congressional district. On the other hand, in New Zealand, seats are set aside exclusively for voters of Maori descent. In both countries, there were dramatic increases in minority representation in national legislatures in the late 1990s (Buenagua, 2010).

Meanwhile, Ager (2008) viewed party list as a part of the electoral process that enables small political parties and marginalized and underrepresented to obtain possible representation not only in the society but also in the Congress where the legislative process occurs.

Party List in the Philippines

Under Party list mode of representation, any national, regional or sectoral party or organization registered with the Commission on Elections (ComElec) may participate in the election process of the Party list representatives who, upon their election and proclamation, shall sit in the House of Representatives as regular members.

However, in ComElec Resolution No. 3307, the following are only allowed to participate according to its Section 3 and these are only the Sectoral Party, Sectoral Organization, Political Party and Coalition.

First, the sectoral party is an organized group of citizens whose principal advocacy pertains to the special interests and concerns of the following sectors: Labor; Peasant; Urban Poor; Indigenous Cultural Communities; Elderly; Handicapped; Women; Youth; Overseas Workers; Fisher folks; Veterans; and Professionals;

Next, sectoral organization on the other hand, is a group of qualified voters bound together by similar physical attributes or characteristics, or by employment, interests or concerns;

Another, political party is an organized group of qualified voters pursuing the same ideology, political ideas and principles for the general conduct of the government; and

Lastly, the Coalition which is an aggrupation of duly-registered national, regional, sectoral parties or organizations for political and/or election purposes.

Scope of Sectoral Party

In scope, a sectoral party, sectoral organization, political party or coalition, may either be national, as when its constituency is spread over the geographical territory of at least a majority of the regions; or regional as when its constituency is spread over the geographical territory of at least a majority of the cities and provinces comprising a region.

In most democratic countries like the Philippines, representing the marginalized or underrepresented sectors of the society was an important matter. 13 years after the first Party-list election, 22 years after the passage of the

Party- list Act, and 30 years after the amendment of the Constitution, it led the country to have formed various groups and different parties. It gave an opportunity as what the Constitution had vested on the Party lists to be the representatives and be the whistleblowers of the unprivileged sectors.

According to the ComElec's Primer, the Party list System is a mechanism of political representation in the election of representatives to the House of Representatives from marginalized or underrepresented national, regional and sectoral parties, or organizations or coalitions registered with the ComElec. It is part of the electoral process that enables small political parties and marginalized and underrepresented sectors to be represented in Congress, which is traditionally dominated by parties with big political machineries.

Basis of Party List System

Also, the country's Party List System is anchored to Section 5 of Article VI of the 1987 Philippine Constitution. Though usually associated with parliamentary governments in other countries around the world, the Party list system was incorporated in the Constitution as an innovative element into our presidential system of government.

Furthermore, Article VI, Sec. 5 of the Constitution clearly states that, the House of Representatives shall be composed of not more than two hundred and fifty members, unless otherwise fixed by law, who shall be elected from legislative districts apportioned among the provinces, cities, and the Metropolitan Manila area in accordance with the number of their respective inhabitants, and on the basis of a uniform and progressive ratio, and those who, as provided by law, shall be elected through a Party list system of registered national, regional, and sectoral parties or organizations.

Percentage of Party List Representatives

The Party list Representatives shall constitute twenty percent of the total number of representatives. For three consecutive terms after the ratification of this Constitution, one half of the seats allocated to party list representatives shall be filled, as provided by law, by selection or election from the labor, peasant, urban poor, indigenous cultural com-munities, women, youth, and such other sectors as may be provided by law, except the religious sector.

Republic Act No. 7941 or the "Party list System Act of 1995" signed by former Philippine Pres. Fidel Ramos on March 3, 1995 was the result after the

House of Representatives was mandated by the Constitution to rule or govern over the laws regarding the Party list representation in the country. Lower House representatives drafted the R.A No. 7941 with the following elements such as:

First, to enable Filipino citizens belonging to marginalized and under-represented sectors, organizations and parties, and who lack well-defined constituents but who could contribute to the formulation and enactment of appropriate legislation, to become members of the House of Representatives;

Second, the state shall develop and guarantee a full, free and open party system in order to attain the broadest possible representation of party, sectoral or group interests in the House of Representatives"; and

Third is, to enhance their chances to compete for and win seats in the simplest scheme possible.

As per the statute's Declaration of Policy, the State shall promote pro-portional representation in the election of representatives to the House of Representatives through a Party list system of registered national, regional and sectoral parties or organizations or coalitions thereof, which will enable Filipino citizens belonging to marginalized and underrepresented sectors, organizations and parties, and who lack well-defined political constituencies but who could contribute to the formulation and enactment of appropriate legislation that will benefit the nation as a whole, to become members of the House of Representatives.

Towards this end, the State shall develop and guarantee a full, free and open party system in order to attain the broadest possible representation of party, sectoral or group interests in the House of Representatives by enhancing their chances to compete for and win seats in the legislature, and shall provide the simplest scheme possible (Republic Act No. 7941).

Moreover, Soliman M. Santos said that the provision mentioned above is an attempt to institutionalize both sectoral representation in national legislative governance and to show the maturity or evolution of the Party list System in the country. Stated otherwise, it is an attempt towards a politics of sectors, programs and parties and used as a boat of those who are in the marginalized and underepresented sectors or groups in our society so that their voices will be heard.

Jurisprudential Basis of Party List Representatives

In Veterans Federation Party vs. ComElec (1998), Court decreed that the

Party list seats shall be determined pursuant to "Four Inviolable Parameters" and these are: 20 % allocation, 2% threshold, three-seat limit chair and proportional representation.

The (20%) twenty percent allocation is the combined number of all Party list congressmen that shall not exceed twenty percent of the total membership of the House of Representatives, including those elected under the Party list.

Second, the (2%) two percent threshold are only to those parties who garnered a minimum of two percent of the total valid votes cast for the Party list system are qualified and will have a seat in the House of Representatives.

Third, the three-seat limit wherein each qualified Party, regardless of the number of votes they actually obtained, is entitled to a maximum of three seats; that is, one qualifying and two additional seats in Congress.

Finally, proportional representation is the additional seats which a qualified Party is entitled to shall be computed in proportion to their total number of votes.

On the latter, the UP National College of Public Administration and Governance Dean, Dr. Edna Co, in her paper "Is There a Party in the House?", she wrote that, RA 7941 stems from the Constitution's intent to provide social justice and to reduce social inequities by 'diffusing wealth and political power for the common good. Also, according to Christian Monsod (July 16, 2007), he said that the Party list system's intent is to diffuse political power among the people in the society and represent themselves in the Congress. To appreciate how the Party list system was envisioned, they went all the way back to the debates of the 1986 Constitutional Commission, particularly to the question of whether it was going to be a system of representation of the marginalized, or whether it would open itself to other groups such as the major political parties.

The Party list system was envisioned to be a vehicle of democratic representation and social justice for the marginalized and underrepresented sectors or groups. It will also serve as a tool to lead the nation through equality and fairness. That everyone among the Filipino people will have the opportunity to speak out or convey the opinions or emotions they have.

However, as viewed by Aceron (2010), the Party list Act has inherent gaps that constrain its capacity to develop a system where full-fledged political parties can eventually thrive. Its first flaw is its definition of party list groups, which disregards organizational requirements and highlights sectoral and marginalization prerequisites.

Ideally, the party list is supposed to provide that breeding ground for parties; but instead of being national political parties with a national development agenda, party list groups have become very sectoral, thereby losing the prospect of party development through the party list. And instead of further consolidating so as to become a major political force, party list groups continuously split in order to gain more seats.

Party List Advocacies

The main advocacy of every Party list is to represent those in the marginalized and unprivileged sectors in the society so that their voices will be heard in the Congress.

Moreover, these Party lists assert equity towards unity through the bills/ laws and house resolutions they filed and through this, it will nourish the foundation of parity over everyone's diversity.

Another, Party list group supports and enhances the bills/laws filed pertaining to anti-discrimination with regards to the age, race and gender identity. Because of this, it opens so many doors for those in the marginalized/ unrepresented sectors who wanted to help and work for their loved ones.

Bayan Muna Party List Advocacies

Bayan Muna Party list is a multi-sectoral representation that aims to establish a democratic, nationalist and popular government by empowering the people, ensuring their representation and participation in all levels of government decision-making. They assert national sovereignty and independence and protect the national patrimony from foreign domination and control. They also promote a self-reliant and sustainable socio-economic development through the integrated programs of genuine land reform, national industrialization and protection of the environment. They firmly uphold and protect the people's basic human rights and freedoms and ensure justice for all victims of human rights violations. They also improve the social and economic welfare of workers, peasants and other marginalized sectors by providing a comprehensive and progressive program in basic social services and livelihood.

Furthermore, Bayan Muna Party list promotes a national culture that is progressive, patriotic, scientific and popular which develops research and development in science and technology. Also, to guarantee the right to self-determination of the Bangsa Moro, Cordillera and other indigenous peoples and ensure their participation in all matters that directly affects them. They foster a just policy of international relations that is independent, peace-oriented and mutually beneficial to our integrity, security and prosperity as a nation. Likewise, they seek to remove all forms of gender oppression and discrimination against women and promote their full involvement in national affairs and other fields of endeavor (www.makabayan.net).

AKBAYAN Party List Advocacies

On the other hand, Akbayan is also a multi-sectoral Party that primarily stands for program-based politics. They seek to transform the dominant practices of personality-and-patronage-based politics. Also, they aim to break the tradition of shady dealings and horse-trading between and among politicians towards more participatory and rational decision-making in the society.

Moreover, public welfare has been undermined for too long by members of the elite who join government to further vested economic interests. It is Akbayan's hope that through citizens' participation in policy-making, the country's economic environment would become accessible to the general population and not just big corporations. Akbayan also seeks to engage government for better social policies that would include redistributive reforms, delivery of basic services and appropriate safety nets (https://akbayan.org.ph).

CIBAC Party List Advocacies

Next is the Citizen's Battle against Corruption (CIBAC), a multi-sectoral Party which advocates the exposure and prosecution of corrupt public officials and their cronies as well as to advocate transparency and fairness in all dealings by the government at all levels. The people need to have their faith restored in government agencies viewed by many as nothing but crime syndicates out to plunder the country. To this end, CIBAC is proposing to initiate several projects that would act as deterrents to those government officials and personnel who would take advantage of the public's trust.

CIBAC Party list also promotes a socially responsive, democratic political structure for a more effective administration and proper formulation of social, cultural and economic policy at all government levels. It follows that after addressing corruption in the government and all its agencies, these institutions would have more resources to perform their mandated tasks. More resources will certainly make policy implementation much easier, thus the needs of the people will be better met.

Also, they uphold the rule of law and a national philosophy that embodies the aspirations of the people and the nation. CIBAC does not advocate mob rule. While vigilance against corruption must always be foremost on its agenda, it recognizes that only legal and constitutionally permissible measures are the means to enforce that vigilance (www.congress.gov.ph).

KABAYAN Party List Advocacies

Another Party list is the KAlusugan paBAhay at kabuhaYAN (KABAYAN) that promotes the full realization of the economic, social and cultural rights of all Filipinos, particularly the marginalized and underrepresented sectors of the society. Last 2016 national and local election, they decided to add two more representation in the Congress: the Overseas Filipino Workers (OFW's) and those in the educational fields that make their recent acronym "KABAYAN+2".

They believe that the government should uphold every person's right to health, to the provision of accessible, quality and compassionate health services. The Party list pursues legislation that shall ensure universal health insurance coverage, which shall ensure free medical services to the poor and underprivileged Filipinos.

The Party list also pursues legislation for the creation of a Department of Housing to assist homeless Filipinos through a comprehensive housing program that covers housing finance, rationale land use, and active community support to ensure affordable and decent shelter. KABAYAN+2 Party list determinedly promotes capability-building in 'cooperativism' and micro-financing for micro, small and medium enterprises to benefit more families in every community (www.congress.gov.ph).

ACT Teachers Party list Advocacies

After that is the ACT Teachers Party list, a marginalized representation that is highly committed to be the true voice of the country's teachers and is aware of its special role in shaping the minds and values of our children and youth. It pledges to represent, assist and defend teachers and other education workers in advancing our vocation, economic welfare and democratic rights.

The ACT Teachers Party list also pledges to represent, assist and defend teachers and other education workers in advancing our vocation, economic welfare and democratic rights. They believe that the children and youth have the right to an education that inculcates love of country, develops scientific thinking and is attuned to the needs of the majority of the people, especially the marginalized and underrepresented groups (www.makabayan.net).

MAGDALO Party List Advocacies

Finally, the Magdalo Para sa Pilipino Party list (MPPL) is a multi-sectoral Party which advocates change and reforms in the society by policy-making and proposing measures to address the problems of the society. It focuses on promoting good governance, security sector reform, poverty alleviation, citizen engagement, sustainable development and climate change adaptation. Similarly, they are socio-political movement for change and good governance, representing reformist officers and soldiers of the Armed Forces of the Philippines and other reform-minded citizen-volunteers of the Republic of the Philippines (www.magdalo.org).

Party List Functions in the Society

The function of Party list in the society is to pass/formulate laws to help those in the marginalized, underrepresented and unprivileged sectors such as the urban poor, women, youth, indigenous communities, senior citizens, farmers and other marginalized sectors that cannot speak for their opinions in the Congress. In theory, these Party list groups should be the representation of these sectors and should be pushing for their concerns in the Congress.

In the Philippines, where the majority rules, sectors in the minority still have their chance to be heard because Party list groups through their representatives help those in the marginalized/unprivileged sectors by leveling out or representing them in the Congress through the bills/laws they filed.

Party list representation is different from district representation. District representatives are elected locally while Party list representatives are elected nationally. These Party list Representatives will be the face of those in the marginalized sectors in the Congress. Though these two representatives were elected differently, they both have and share the same powers, duties and benefits. They create and sponsor bills, be the head committees, call an investigation and other powers vested to them as a member of the House of Representatives.

Actually, there's no perfect thing in this imperfect world. Some might not easily get the assistance they needed but through Party list Representation, it helps the people in the society to be noticed and be recognized. Moreover, the function of the Party list is to connect people to the government so that they will never be out from reality. In other words, Filipino people will keep updated and they are knowledgeable enough about what to do and where to ask if they need a help.

Tan (2010) viewed that the Party list system was not intended solely for marginalized/unprivileged sectors. It was also intended to empower smaller political parties regardless of sector, particularly those with a substantial following not concentrated in a single district. Constitutional Commissioner Christian Monsod, for example, argued that any group that can muster 500,000 members deserves a House seat. This would allow ideology-based parties such as an environmental party or regional parties for Bicolanos and Warays too weak to contest district seats.

Chief Justice Artemio Panganiban (2010), however, held in a judicial tour de force that the Party list system is solely intended for the marginalized, and the *"national"* and *"regional"* parties must be national and regional parties for the marginalized. He wrote: "The law crafted to address the peculiar disadvantages of Payatas hovel dwellers cannot be appropriated by the mansion owners of Forbes Park." He also added that party-list nominees must be from the sector they represent. Chief Justice Panganiban's formulation in the Ang Bagong Bayani case has gained universal acceptance, especially in the ComElec.

Finally, the constitutional commissioners anticipated that small parties would ally with large ones. In the German system that the likes of Monsod referred to, such alliances split votes between a district candidate and a Party list, given there are two votes as in our system. Such alliances are the very fabric of politics and do not mean a Party list group is an administration front group.

Party List Program Involvement

Party list groups have a huge contribution to the formulation and enactment of appropriate bills/laws that will benefit the nation as a whole. Through their programs inside and outside of the Congress, it shows gradual changes and developments in the society over the period of time. This study focused on Bayan Muna, Akbayan, CIBAC, KABAYAN+2, ACT TEACHERS and MAGDALO Parties.

BAYAN MUNA Party List Program Involvement

First, Bayan Muna Party list in which they prioritize more the general welfare of the Filipino people above everything else through their programs and services. They also fight for justice, peace and democracy in the country. Bayan Muna represents many different sectors from the poor, laborers, indigenous people, peasants and even fisher folks that are why they are classified as multi- sectoral Party.

Since Bayan Muna is considered as an old and adept Party list in the Philippines, they have already sponsored numerous bills and house resolutions in the Congress, 298 to be exact. Among of these are the R.A. 9745 also known as 'Anti-Torture Law' which penalizes any forms of torture including physical, emotional, and the like. Together with GABRIELA Women's Party list, Bayan Muna supported R.A. 9262 or the 'Violence Against Women and Children Act' (VAWC). Furthermore, they also sponsored the R.A. 9504 or the 'Tax Relief for Minimum Wage Earners Act of 2008'.

With all the achievements of Bayan Muna, they still continue to strive for change through their efforts intended to help those in the marginalized/unprivileged sectors and one of these includes the desire to help the Bangsa Moro people to achieve self-determination; help to improve the lives of indigenous people, give justice to those who are victims of human rights violation, help in the preservation of the environment, help in addressing and raising the important issues of the oppressed and many more (www.makabayan.net).

AKBAYAN Party list Program Involvement

Secondly, Akbayan Party list seeks to engage government for better social policies that would include redistributive reforms, delivery of basic services and appropriate safety nets. They authored 102 bills/laws in the Congress among them is the passage of Cheaper and Quality Medicines Law, Comprehensive Agrarian Reform Program Extension with Reforms (CARPER) Law and the Republic Act 10354 or Responsible Parenthood and Reproductive Health Law, which guarantees universal access to methods of contraception, fertility control, sexual education, and maternal care.

Moreover, Akbayan seeks to contribute to the development of a political party system that is based on programs and accountabilities, and not on political opportunism. It envisions a political culture where citizens are genuinely aware, responsive and free. Through their program involvement, it involves the Filipino people in decision-making and in legislative process (https://akbayan.org.ph).

CIBAC Party List Program Involvement

Next one is the Citizens' Battle against Corruption Party list (CIBAC), which was dedicated towards fighting graft, corruption and cronyism inside the government. Almost 44 pending and passed bills/laws filed/proposed by CIBAC Party list and they are the brain behind the passages of 'Anti-Red Tape Act', 'Anti-Marital Infidelity Act', 'Anti-Smuggling Act', and the creation of Public Attorney's Office (PAO). CIBAC continue to provide good quality of programs/services to their constituents through scholarship, hospitalization, livelihood and nationwide feeding programs. They envisions a corruption-free Philippines and giving worthy services to Filipinos (www.congress.gov.ph).

KABAYAN Party List Program Involvement

KABAYAN+2 envisions that every Filipino workers will live with dignity in a democratic and humane society. It aims to protect peoples' rights and promote peoples' welfare, provide opportunities for peoples' health, shelter, growth and development, and pave the way for a just, equal, and free society. They filed 102 (both passed and pending) bills/laws in the Congress since they were elected in 2016.

Likewise, they authored the Universal Health Care System for all Filipinos and they are among the principal authors of R.A 8239 aka "Extending the Validity of Passport from 5 years to 10 years". KABAYAN+2 also authored the 3C Basic Education System on the development of Critical Thinking, Craftsmanship and Character in the Philippines. Through the programs/services they offered, it nourishes and secures the lives of every Filipinos (www.congress.gov.ph).

ACT Teachers Party List Program Involvement

Fifth, as the real voice of teachers, the ACT Teachers Party list supports and fights for three major points: first, the economic rights and welfare of teachers and educational staff; second, relevant reforms in the educational system; and third, good governance. They also focuses on the development of every Filipino teachers in the country. But as time goes by, this Party list offers programs and services for youth sectors concerning good quality of education. They authored 225 (both passed and pending) bills/laws in the Congress and more of these pertain to the teachers (www.makabayan.com).

MAGDALO Party List Program Involvement

Lastly, Magdalo Para sa Pilipino (For The People) Party list that helps the veteran soldiers in war and the current security workers in the Philippines such as policemen, armed forces and the navy through the bills they filed and proposed. They authored almost 262 (passed and pending bills) which aims to increase the quality of facilities and their salaries and also to develop insurances and benefits they get from the government. Among of these are House Bill No. 107 aka "An Act Establishing the Filipino Identification System", House Bill No. 1122 or "An Act providing for a Magna Carta of the Poor", House Bill No. 2723 aka "An Act creating the Department of Maritime Affairs providing funds therefor and for other purposes" and the House Bill No. 6149 or the "An Act providing for an Increase in the Standing Force of the Armed Forces of the Philippines through the Recruitment and Special Enlistment of Provisional Enlisted Personnel" (www.magdalo.org).

3
METHODOLOGY

This chapter discussed the methods of research used, population frame and sampling, description of the respondent, data gathering procedure, instruments used and statistical treatment used.

Research Method Used

The method used in the study is a qualitative descriptive method using narrative approach. According to Lambert, C and Lambert, V (2012), it is an approach that is very useful when researchers want to know, regarding events, who were involved, what was involved, and where did things take place. Narrative approach as cited in "Spoken Stories" by Valli (2012) is a form of inquiry in which the researchers studied the lives of individuals and asks one or more individuals to provide stories about their lives. The narrative combines views from the participant's life with those of the researchers' life in a collaborative narrative.

Population Frame and Sampling Scheme

The population of the study was composed of six (6) respondents. The respondents were classified as Party List Representatives in the Congress. Purposive sampling was used to collect data from the six respondents.

Description of the Respondents

The respondents of the study were the representatives of Party List in the Congress such as: Cong. Carlos Isagani Zarate of Bayan Muna Party List, Cong. Tom Villarin of Akbayan Party List, Cong. Sherwin Tugna of CIBAC Party List, Cong. Ron Salo of KABAYAN Party List, Cong. Antonio Tinio of Act Teachers Party List and Cong. Gary Alejano of Magdalo Para sa Pilipino Party List.

First, Carlos Isagani "Kaloi" Tabora Zarate is a member of the Philippine House of Representatives, representing Bayan Muna Party list. Zarate engaged in a small legal practice focused on human rights law, serving a wide clientele including laborers, small farmers, indigenous peoples (Lumads) including the Moro, urban poor, and political prisoners. Zarate also served on various capacities on different professional associations for lawyers.

Second, Tomasito "Tom" Villarin of Akbayan Party list is a student activist in Manila at the height of the anti-Marcos struggle in the 80s. After receiving his A.B. Economics degree from the University of Santo Tomas, he immediately worked with the labor movement as an energetic trade union organizer and educator. In Mindanao, Tom involved himself with governance and democratization work, peace building in conflict areas, promoting sustainable agriculture and social enterprise development among farming communities.

Third, Sherwin Tugna is a three-term Filipino congressman who represented the Citizens' Battle Against Corruption (CIBAC) Party list group in the 15th,16th, and 17th Congresses of the Philippines. Tugna would go on to become one of the Assistant Majority Leaders of the 15th Congress. He presently sits as the Chairman of the House Committee on Suffrage and Electoral Reforms. He is one of the lead prosecutors during the historic impeachment trial of Chief Justice Renato Corona.

Fourth, Atty. Ron Perez Salo is a public sector consultant of the Department of Health, Food and Drug Administration, National Nutrition Council and Development Academy of the Philippines on various legal and policy matters. He is also a Law professor at the UP College of Law & La Salle College of Law. Salo served as assistant secretary at the Office of the Legislative Adviser from 2006 to 2009, and undersecretary at the Office of the Executive Secretary from 2009 to 2010.

Fifth, Antonio "Tonchi" Tinio is a Filipino activist and member of the House of Representatives (congressman), sitting as representative of ACT Teachers Party list from the 15th to the 17th (current) Congress, serving as

Assistant Minority Floor Leader in the 15th Congress. He was the national chairperson of the Alliance of Concerned Teachers (ACT) from 2002 to 2012. At present, under his chairmanship, the Committee on Public Information approved the Freedom of Information Bill. He is a member of Committee on Basic Education and eight other committees.

Last, Gary Cajolo Alejano Sr. is a former captain in the Philippine Marine Corps. He became involved in the Oakwood incident in 2003 and later, in the Manila Peninsula siege. His involvement in these protests led to his incarceration for almost four years. Inside detention, they formed the Magdalo Para sa Pagbabago Movement (MPPM) and organized the Samahang Magdalo, Inc. (SMI) under it.

Instrument Used

The instrument used by the researchers in the study is a focus group discussion and in-depth interview using interview sheet questionnaires consists of six interview questions with follow up questions.

Data Gathering Procedure

The process of gathering of data was not easy because the chosen respondents were elected representatives of Party list and working on the Congress. Researchers had requested an appointment for an interview in the respective party list offices hoping that they would respond positively and consider the request. Luckily, most offices agreed though series of phone calls were made.

Prior to that, researchers secured and sent a letter of requests to their emails along with interview questionnaires. Aside from letters, the researchers conducted follow-up calls. When the researchers received the approvals, interview was conducted at the time agreed upon. The interviews were conducted at respondent's offices in Congress. The proper manner of interviewing was observed, considering that the respondents are political figures as elected representatives.

Data Analysis

Data was analyzed through descriptive and narrative reports. Answers from each representative were involved. Data collected was interpreted.

Analysis was done through literature review and inferences from the researchers.

4

RESULTS AND DISCUSSION

This chapter presents the data obtained from the respondents as well as from books, readings and articles, including the analysis and interpretation.

Political Representation

1. What is the political representation of the party list system?

A. To be specific, what sector your party representing?

Hon. Sherwin Tugna (CIBAC Party list Representative):

"According to the decision of the Supreme Court, party list groups are not merely limited to marginalize sectors there can be a sectoral or multi sectoral organization that can be a party list." Citizens Battle against Corruption is an organization composed of different individuals whose common and united advocacy and aspiration and our goal here is Government is to promote anti-corruption and to promote good governance. CIBAC party list falls under the category of multi sectoral organization."

Hon. Tom Villarin (AKBAYAN Party list Representative):

"Akbayan or the Citizens Action Party politically is a multi- sectoral organization it is by nature it's a political party because under our party list

system of representation it's either political party or a sectoral party that join in the party list system election. We represent different sectors such as labor, farmers, women, LGBT and youth."

Hon. Ron Salo (KABAYAN Party list Representative):

"Kabayan party list is multi sector party, were have members from youth, urban poor, rural poor, we also have OFWs we also have some professionals including teachers government workers, seafarers, we even have tricycle driver."

Hon. Antonio Tinio (ACT TEACHERS Party list Representative):

"We represent teachers, education sector employees and all interested in education. Hon. Carlos Isagani Zarate (BAYANMUNA Party list Representative): Bayan Muna is a multi-sectoral political party, it represents no particular sector because under R.A 7941 or the Party list System, it allows sectoral party or sectoral organization or political party. Because of this, we deal with a variety of issues confronting our marginalized sectors."

Hon. Gary Alejano (MAGDALO Party list Representative):

"Magdalo party list is a sectoral representation. It is not a political party. The Magdalo aims to represent the former or retired members of AFP and of course the urban poor and youth. But in reality not only those two sectors."

B. Do you belong to the group that you represent?

Hon. Sherwin Tugna (CIBAC Party list Representative):

"Yes, when I was the attorney of our party. We filed a case and joined the public protest of the newly elected President Joseph Estrada."

Hon. Tom Villarin (AKBAYAN Party list Representative):

"Prior to me being elected in Akbayan as there representative, I was in NGO (non- government organization) sector. I was with the farmers in Mindanao and prior to that, I was also a student activist in my college days in the 80's. I also was with the unions after I graduate college. I work

in trade union I was labor organizer."

Hon. Ron Salo (KABAYAN Party list Representative):

"Yes, as a professional, but at the same time, as a government worker because I have been working with the government since I was a student. As a law student, I was once a member of a staff here in the Congress."

Hon. Antonio Tinio (ACT TEACHERS Party list Representative):

"Yes, I am a teacher."

Hon. Carlos Isagani Zarate (BAYANMUNA Party list Representative):

"Of course you cannot effectively represent or be the voice of the marginalized or poor if you do not belong to that sector. I think it should be a requirement in any Party list that you should belong to the group you represent. It's impossible that you have a tricycle driver or security guard Party list and you are not a tricycle driver or security guard yourself."

Hon. Gary Alejano (MAGDALO Party list Representative):

"Yes, I'm a former soldier of the Armed Forces as part of Philippine Marine."

C. As you represent those sector what is your priority?

Hon. Sherwin Tugna (CIBAC Party list Representative):

"If you will check the legislative records, the bills filed by CIBAC are majority anti- corruption like strengthening the Ombudsman Act and bills that provide funds to whistle blowers and those who engage in corruption."

Hon. Tom Villarin (AKBAYAN Party list Representative):

"In terms of priority, all sectors have priority legislative advocacies."

Hon. Ron Salo (KABAYAN Party list Representative):

"Not exactly what specific area or sector should I prioritize it's really more of advocacies, we call Kabayan plus 2, first is Kalusugan (Health), Pabahay (Housing), Kabuhayan (Livelihood), so that's why Kabayan, plus

Edukasyon (Education) and OFWs (Overseas Filipino Workers)."

Hon. Antonio Tinio (ACT TEACHERS Party list Representative):

"Our priority is especially on Teachers and other sectors of education."

Hon. Carlos Isagani Zarate (BAYANMUNA Party list Representative):

"Since BAYANMUNA Party list is multi-sectoral; we prioritize the up-holding of our by-laws. Then we are pushing for resolution of our foreign capitalist-driven country and the betterment of our countrymen. Our priority since we entered the Congress in 2001 is comprehensive and effective Agrarian Reform Laws; from proper orientation of the People's Mining Bill to laws that will push country-wide industrialization, because we believe that will lead to our progress."

Hon. Gary Alejano (MAGDALO Party list Representative):

"Our priority is security sector reform. The Magdalo group performed a coup d'etat because of problem in the government and corruption. We have major policy plans, good governance, anti-corruption, security sector reforms, sustainable development, and we pursue reform on our environmental laws. We also represent the war veterans."

D. When did you realize that you want to represent this kind of sector/s in the Congress?

D.1 What is the first thing you do after your Party earned seat/s in the Congress? And how do you feel about that?

Hon. Sherwin Tugna (CIBAC Party list Representative):

"Way back in 2008-2009, I was already part of the party (as a lawyer) although in a different capacity. What we like is proper appropriation of government funds. This is my last term as Congressman, so we really lack time. First we review the bill that we need to file, and then we coordinate with the anti-corruption and good governance group. We also go to the Mayors and Barangay Captains (County leaders) for feedback on effectiveness of our legislation in terms of corruption and good governance."

Hon. Tom Villarin (AKBAYAN Party list Representative):

"AKBAYAN was founded in 1998. I was an original founder and worked in the farmers' sector. The trend is critical to the political system personally financed by billionaires. Akbayan was founded in the belief of meaningful electoral reform as early in 1998. Akbayan won the first Party list in 1998 election, since then AKBAYAN was represented in the Congress. The first representative was Cong. Etta Rosales, which advocates on human rights. This is my first time in Congress representing AKBAYAN."

Hon. Ron Salo (KABAYAN Party list Representative):

"I am the founder of this Party list, I was encourage to put up this Party list after I represented the Philippine government in Geneva on migrant workers. What we did immediately after the proclamation is to gather stakeholders: the officers, the members and the supporters, in order for us to talk out the proposed measures that were going to file here in Congress."

Hon. Antonio Tinio (ACT TEACHERS Party list Representative):

"We decided back in 2009 to form this Party list to join the 2010 election. Of course we filed bills based on the concerns of teachers. Before entering the Congress, I was a long time teacher and activist in the Education sector."

Hon. Carlos Isagani Zarate (BAYANMUNA Party list Representative):

"Personally, I don't have any plans in Congress, but I have been party of BAYANMUNA since 2001. Back in 1999, I was already a practicing lawyer as human rights lawyer. I stated in BAYANMUNA as legal-council in Mindanao, eventually I was nominated in 2012 as second nominee of the party. Fortunately, BAYANMUNA gained two seats in the Congress so I was included. When I entered the Congress in 2013, the current treding issue is pork barrel funds, so our legislation was focused there. We joined the People's Initiative against Pork (PIP) calling for initiative and invoking the law and to abolish the pork barrel."

Hon. Gary Alejano (MAGDALO Party list Representative):

"Actually we are forced by circumstances in politics. We immediately laid down all our legislative agenda."

Discussion:

The Political representation of the Party list system in the Philippines shows that it can be a sectoral parties or organizations or coalitions as long as they belong to the marginalized and underrepresented sectors, organizations and parties that could contribute to the formulation and enactment of legislation that will benefit the nation (Republic Act 7941).

Majority of the respondents in this study belongs to the organization that represents multisectoral or many different sectors in the Congress.

Prior to their election as a Party list representative of their groups, they belong to the group that they represent like Cong. Villarin of Akbayan, which is a former representative of NGO's sector; Cong. Alejano, which is a former Marine; Cong. Tinio, which is a teacher; Cong. Zarate and Cong. Tugna as the former lawyer of their party; or the one who formed the group such as Cong. Salo, which is the brain for the formation of KABAYAN Party list. Thus, the representative knows the real advocacies, functions, programs of their respective group.

According to the representatives, they realized their Party was formed to have a "*new politics*" where their Party list was formed to reflect the move towards program-based politics rather than on personalities and traditional; to have a meaningful electoral reform where aim to increase the representation, particularly of marginalized and underrepresented sectors and enhance transparency and accountability leading to more efficient government.

Advocacies of Party List

2. What are the advocacies, functions and programs of selected party list system?

    2.1 What is your Party's main advocacy?

        2.1.A If _____ is your main advocacy, are there any advocacies for other sector/s you represent? Can you enumerate them?

Hon. Sherwin Tugna (CIBAC Party list Representative):

"*Anti- corruption, Citizen Battle Against Corruption.*"

Hon. Tom Villarin (AKBAYAN Party list Representative):

"Well basically protection, promotion of human rights as a universal value; and the promotion of human rights. It should be reflected on the sectoral advocacies."

Hon. Ron Salo (KABAYAN Party list Representative):

"KABAYAN stands for Kalusugan (Health), Pabahay (Housing) at Kabu-hayan (Livelihood). Then we have KABAYAN + 2, Edukasyon (Education) and OFW (Overseas Filipino Worker). These are the focus of KABAYAN Party list."

Hon. Antonio Tinio (ACT TEACHERS Party list Representative):

"Education, Rights and Improvement of teachers. Advocate and Rights to Education of every Filipino. To fight for a just, equal, democratic, peaceful and progressive nation."

Hon. Carlos Isagani Zarate (BAYANMUNA Party list Representative):

"The main advocacy of BAYANMUNA (Nation First) since it joined the Congress back in 2001 is to advance the causes of the marginalized sector."

Hon. Gary Alejano (MAGDALO Party list Representative):

"More on security sector reforms. Then we also advocate good governance, sustainable development and climate change adaptation."

> 2.1.B What are the steps your Party is taking to accomplish those advocacies you mentioned above?

Hon. Sherwin Tugna (CIBAC Party list Representative):

"Research, talk to others and civil society organization that has the same interest and same advocacies."

Hon. Tom Villarin (AKBAYAN Party list Representative):

"We have consultations and involvement with the Legislation.

Hon. Ron Salo (KABAYAN Party list Representative):

"We have regular meeting with the board members of the party, then have a talk with the stakeholders."

Hon. Antonio Tinio (ACT TEACHERS Party list Representative):

"We have consultation with the stakeholders."

Hon. Carlos Isagani Zarate (BAYANMUNA Party list Representative):

"We have consultation with our members and organization under the BayanMuna Party list."

Hon. Gary Alejano (MAGDALO Party list Representative):

"Well, we have meetings with the members, which legislative agenda should we pushed through. We also have dissemination of information in the Magdalo group."

Discussion:

The researchers considered that most advocacies of certain Party list aim to provide a better living for Filipinos, through transparent and fair government and the full realization of the economic, social and cultural rights of Filipinos. Most answer of the representatives concluded that their advocacies would bring the concerns of marginalized or multi sectoral groups into the agenda of both the government and the general public. There advocacies also support change and reforms in the society through policy making and proposing measures to address the problems of the society (De Asis, Flores and Navarro, 2010).

Functions of the Party list in the Congress

2.2 How does your Party works in the Congress?

2.2.A What is the role of your party inside or outside of the Congress?

Hon. Sherwin Tugna (CIBAC Party list Representative):

"You can be the best speaker here always delivering bombastic privilege speech but it does not necessarily turn into votes, so we go to different towns and barangays and talk to to different civil society organization. We also speak to a mass of people like, for example, students and talk about good governance. It is to the benefit of our country and citizens and how progress is achieved when there is good governance."

Hon. Tom Villarin (AKBAYAN Party list Representative):

"AKBAYAN remained consistent as a fiscalizer in the Administration. We are the foremost human rights champion. We also carry the interest of the basic sectors. It is proven by the bills we passed. Outside Congress, we have organized protest against abuses from the government and corruption."

Hon. Ron Salo (KABAYAN Party list Representative):

"I am member of several committees (around 14 committees) and two of which as the Vice-Chair. Inside Congress, I'm attending a lot of committee hearings, sessions and meetings with people; more or less meeting with various departments pursuing the advocacies of Kabayan Party list. Outside the Congress, we usually go to other places pursuing our projects."

Hon. Antonio Tinio (ACT TEACHERS Party list Representative):

"Inside the Congress, our main duty is to uphold and defend the interest of the Filipinos, not only the teachers. We participate in different activities, such as budget hearings. Outside the Congress, it's the same. We consult with our constituents, who are active in rallies and political dialogues."

Hon. Carlos Isagani Zarate (BAYANMUNA Party list Representative):

"BAYANMUNA have different Chapters all over the Philippines. With them, our advocacies are disseminated all over the Philippines."

Hon. Gary Alejano (MAGDALO Party list Representative):

"Inside proposing bills, create laws. Outside, we engage heavily with the Armed Forces retired sectors. Then community works inside the govern-

ment. We engage in different activities, such as tree planting. We represent the people, whatever their welfare is, we pursue them. It is also our responsibility to educate the people about the issues in the government."

> 2.2.B Aside from creating or proposing bills/ laws for the sector/s, what else are the other things that you're Party is doing to help your constituents/ members to be more productive and well-function to our community?

Hon. Sherwin Tugna (CIBAC Party list Representative):

"We have academic scholarships, free legal aid and medical assistance."

Hon. Tom Villarin (AKBAYAN Party list Representative):

"Our main program is organizing which is based on territorial level, starting in the Barangay (county). In the Barangay level, interest of the community starts, like the farmers and workers. In the youth sector, counseling of students, guidance of the out-of-school youth and academic scholarship. We passed a bill for free tuition in College level."

Hon. Carlos Isagani Zarate (BAYANMUNA Party list Representative):

"We have programs for academic scholarships and medical mission."

Hon. Gary Alejano (MAGDALO Party list Representative):

"We have scholarship, medical assistance and community works like tree planting and housing projects for AFP (Armed Forces of the Philippines) and PNP (Philippine National Police)."

> 2.2.C Do you think your members/constituents appreciate the efforts and presence of your Party? Do you have any data that will support your claim? Can we have a copy of it?

Hon. Sherwin Tugna (CIBAC Party list Representative):

"I believe yes, most especially our youth; they are very much aware of what is happening in our country. We gave several academic scholarships and livelihood programs. The people involved are very appreciative and grateful."

Hon. Tom Villarin (AKBAYAN Party list Representative):

"Yes, the laws that we passed are for our advocates, which represent their sectors like the peasant caucus and the farmers that marched from Bukidnon to Manila as protest In terms of data, having been reelected in every election that is the primary proof that AKBAYAN is supported."

Hon. Ron Salo (KABAYAN Party list Representative):

"Of course yes, I believe we have the support of our constituents. What we do usually is meeting with the board; we have regular meetings sometimes twice or thrice. Number 2, we have a social media account which most members show their encouragement."

Hon. Carlos Isagani Zarate (BAYANMUNA Party list Representative):

"We haven't conducted a survey yet. The fact that we here in Congress since 2001 is a proof that we are appreciated."

Hon. Gary Alejano (MAGDALO Party list Representative):

"We haven't had any surveys yet. Regarding the second question, we felt we are appreciated because we are still elected by the people."

2.2.D Are there any instances that your Party failed to do most especially in proposing/legislating certain laws in the Congress?

Hon. Sherwin Tugna (CIBAC Party list Representative):

"Yes"

Hon. Tom Villarin (AKBAYAN Party list Representative):

"Well, not all the bills that we proposed are being pushed through, which is frustrating for us. The whole process is very political because each representative, even the President, is loyal with their political party. Example is the Agrarian Reform Bill, which received a lot of resistance because of several land-owners which are politicians on the first place. You really have to compromise."

Hon. Ron Salo (KABAYAN Party list Representative):

"So far none."

Hon. Carlos Isagani Zarate (BAYANMUNA Party list Representative):

"We have a lot. Actually we have a list here, but a lot of it are also in process."

Hon. Gary Alejano (MAGDALO Party list Representative):

"Yes. First we have to take a look at the legislative agenda of the administration. Second, we have to look at the legislative priority of the leaders in Congress and the chairmen of the committee. If it's not their priority, then nothing will happen."

2.2.E Why do you think you fail?

Hon. Sherwin Tugna (CIBAC Party list Representative):

"In reality the whole process is not smooth sailing. You will really encounter resistance against your bill, especially if the majority in Congress does not like it. It is very political."

Hon. Tom Villarin (AKBAYAN Party list Representative):

"We have a lot of politicians with personal vested interests. Most of them are millionaires, landlords, and lawyers of big corporation. These are the people that you will face when you propose bills."

Hon. Carlos Isagani Zarate (BAYANMUNA Party list Representative):

"The Congress is very conservative. They resist change, especially comprehensive reforms. What they support are bills that is in favor of their personal interest."

Hon. Gary Alejano (MAGDALO Party list Representative):

"The bills are not part of their legislative agenda."

Discussion:

The researchers sum up the main functions of Party list inside the Congress are simply legislate laws, attend committee hearings, attend daily session and meet with different people and heads of different government agencies. Party list representatives are allowed also to head a standing committee in the Congress, as long as they are member of Majority group in the House, such as Cong. Tugna which is the head of Suffrage and Electoral Reform and Cong. Salo as an Assistant Majority Leader and Vice Chairperson of Education and Rural Development; while the other party list representatives are part of the Minority group. They are not allowed to head a committee, but simply just a member of a committee (Grande, 2016).

On the contrary their functions outside the Congress are to go to other places pursuing projects that part of their advocacies; talk to different leaders of towns, barangays, and civil society organization to tackle different issues concerning their sectors. The three respondents (Bayan Muna, Akbayan, and ACT TEACHERS) are active in the streets, engaging in direct action of a variety of people's issues and concerns.

Functions of Party List as To Bills Filed and Reform in Party List Law

2.3 What is the status of your current bill? Are there any support coming from other legislators?

2.3.A Is there any pending bill your Party filed/ proposed in the Congress to support your Party's program involvement?

Hon. Sherwin Tugna (CIBAC Party list Representative):

"Some are in the second and third reading."

Hon. Tom Villarin (AKBAYAN Party list Representative):

"Yes, we have a lot of legislative bills."

Hon. Ron Salo (KABAYAN Party list Representative):

"Yes, a lot."

Hon. Antonio Tinio (ACT TEACHERS Party list Representative):

"We have a lot. You can check the list."

Hon. Carlos Isagani Zarate (BAYAN MUNA Party list Representative):

"We have a lot of bills filed. Some are being re-filed."

Hon. Gary Alejano (MAGDALO Party list Representative):

"We have a lot of bills. Some are in the second and third reading. Some are even enacted as laws. Magdalo pary is the second most productive party in the seventeenth Congress, third in the whole Congress history."

2.3.B What appropriate policy would you propose in order to achieve reform in our current Party list System?

2.3.B.4 We know that we have 4 inviolable parameters in electing Party list members: 2% threshold, three seat-limit chair, 20% allocation and proportional representation. If you have given a chance to amend or reform any of the 4 inviolable parameters, what would it be? Why?

Hon. Sherwin Tugna (CIBAC Party list Representative):

"Actually all is in order. It's up to the people whether to vote for or not to vote. Honestly, I think it's good, I mean a lot of people are saying we have to reform the Party list system, but in reality the way to reform it is for people to vote for whom they believe are performing well and not to vote for those who are not performing well."

Hon. Tom Villarin (AKBAYAN Party list Representative):

"First, is to define and uphold the marginalized sector. Second is broader political reform. Like 50% Party list representative and 50% from political parties."

Hon. Ron Salo (KABAYAN Party list Representative):

"They have to ensure the "legitimate Party list", so it's a question on how to ensure that the party list will not go bastardize meaning legitimate groups or sector are being represented. Also the 2%, it's not viable anymore. Because the 2% allotted in the Congress for Party list is only almost 50 representatives. We have 68 Party list members; a lot will be left out."

Hon. Antonio Tinio (ACT TEACHERS Party list Representative):

"Well we should define first what is marginalized. The latest Supreme Court ruling opened the Party list to everyone, not only the marginalized sectors, but even to regional sectors. Also, they have to remove the maximum of three seats in order for it to become more proportional. Even the 2% threshold, they have to reform it."

Hon. Carlos Isagani Zarate (BAYAN MUNA Party list Representative):

"They should follow what is stated in the Constitution that the Party list will serve the marginalized sector. Everything changed when the Supreme Court opened the Party list not only to the marginalized. We would like to amend the Party list again to be exclusive for marginalized sector. What we really like is to have a truthful and transparent representation of the marginalized sector. Because now anybody could be a candidate for Party list, even the rich can represent, which is not the aim of Party list. What the Supreme Court should do is to amend the threshold of 2%."

Hon. Gary Alejano (MAGDALO Party list Representative):

"Actually in the last Congress we propose a reform in the Party list. It didn't push through. Aside from proportional representation, reform should truly happen. The representation of the marginalized is not really happening because in reality, the Party list is just an extension of political dynasties. The 20% allocation is actually okay. 2% is already enough. It should be implemented strictly. Proportional representation should be observed because it will just be toppled with bogus Party list. The 3 seats rule is also okay. The real problems are the proper representation of the Party list and its accreditation in ComElec."

Discussion:

It shows that more bills filed by the party list representative are on the second and third reading, some bills are on the committee level and other has been substituted by other bills (Antiquerra and Mangilit, 2010). Even that there are bills filed to support their advocacies; it is hard to pass the bill because of the self-interest of some lawmakers who belonging to the political families and oligarch groups. The researchers also concluded that the bills principally sponsored clearly reflect the political and social constituencies from which they came from. Congressman Zarate's and Congressman Villarin's bills reflect their strong constituency with the urban poor, agricultural sector, and human rights. Congressman Tugna reflects more on anti-corruption. Congressman Tinio reflects more on the concerns of the education. Congressman Salo and Congressman Alejano reflect their organization campaign for reform and change in government.

In terms of policy about the current Party list system or the Republic Act 7941, the respondents are satisfied with the current features defined in the law such as the twenty percent allocation of the total number of representatives. Next is the proportional representation. Third, the two percent threshold and lastly, the three seats limit rule.

However, some Party list representative said that the party list system is bastardized because even the traditional and big political group dominates the Party list system. Some representatives do not come from the sector they advocate but from wealthy political families which are already over represented. They said that the current Party list should strengthen and limit only to the marginalized and underrepresented sectors in the society because the party list is being abused (Tan, 2010).

To sum up, the Party list representatives want that the party list to focus only on the representation of the marginalized and underrepresented sectors of the society.

Rules and Regulations in the Party's Organization

2.4 Do you have internal rules and regulations that should be followed by your Party members?

2.4.A Are you that type of leader who's very strict in implementing your Party's rules and regulations?

Hon. Tom Villarin (AKBAYAN Party list Representative):

"As a political party we have a Constitution and by-laws. We also have Code of Ethics that should be followed."

Hon. Ron Salo (KABAYAN Party list Representative):

"Yes of course. Partly yes, partly no. Party yes in those matters that are non-negotiable. There are some principles that are negotiable. There I'm strict."

Hon. Antonio Tinio (ACT TEACHERS Party list Representative):

"Yes, we have Constitution and by-laws needed to be followed."

Hon. Carlos Isagani Zarate (BAYAN MUNA Party list Representative):

"I am the Executive Vice-President, in terms of discipline. All is processed under executive council."

Hon. Gary Alejano (MAGDALO Party list Representative):

"Yes, we are strict and we adhere to our Code of Ethics. Next, we have core values especially loyalty. If you have a violation, we will dismiss you."

2.4.B How do you give punishments to those who violate your Party's rules and regulations and do you give them such consideration/ second chances for them to correct their mistakes?

Hon. Tom Villarin (AKBAYAN Party list Representative):

"Those members who don't support the advocacy of the party are dismissed. You have to live by the principles of AKBAYAN."

Hon. Ron Salo (KABAYAN Party list Representative):

"Yes we have expelled a number of members. One of those is Harry Roque. We exercise "wait gratitude", meaning we tolerate the menial misbehav-

iors, but we use extreme measures on grave instances.

Hon. Antonio Tinio (ACT TEACHERS Party list Representative):

"Yes we are strict. We follow our Constitution and by-laws."

Hon. Carlos Isagani Zarate (BAYAN MUNA Party list Representative):

"We follow due process here. Not because I'm their representative, I have the last say on the matter. We articulate our point of view and have a dialogue on issues."

Hon. Gary Alejano (MAGDALO Party list Representative):

"We go through deliberations on grave cases. We dismiss the member if proven guilty."

Discussion:

Many of those Party list representatives said that there are the leaders of their respective parties acted as a Chairman and President. According to them, the rules and regulations of their party are based on the approved Constitution and by-laws of their party that agreed upon during their Party Congress. The reason given by the Party list representative, as a leader, why they give punishment to their members is because of disloyalty, dishonorable behavior and violation of Party's constitution and laws.

Party List Preparation, Planning and Analyzing

3. How does your party list prepare, plan and analyze? Do you consult your benefactors?

   3.1 What are the preparations that your Party is doing in proposing bills/laws and how prepared is your Party for the possible outcomes whether it's negative or positive?

       3.1.A How does your Party formulate the bills/laws that will be proposed in the Congress? Did you just base it in your own perception or to the beneficiary constituents?

Hon. Tom Villarin (AKBAYAN Party list Representative):

"In preparation, we have Party Congress one year before the election. There we present the general Plan of Action. We invite the constituents in the committee hearing."

Hon. Ron Salo (KABAYAN Party list Representative):

"We have a meeting with our board, we consult our benefactors."

Hon. Antonio Tinio (ACT TEACHERS Party list Representative):

"We usually do consultation on different regions, mostly teachers. We report our accomplishments to them and we listen to their concerns."

Hon. Carlos Isagani Zarate (BAYAN MUNA Party list Representative):

"We consult our constituents and beneficiaries. Example we consulted the health workers when we filed the Anti- Privatization of Public Hospitals."

Hon. Gary Alejano (MAGDALO Party list Representative):

"In terms of preparation, we consult our constituents."

> 3.1.B What method of referral you made? Did you just present it to them with discussion or you just conducted a survey first before you draft it?

Hon. Tom Villarin (AKBAYAN Party list Representative):

"Focus group discussion, regional consultation, sectoral caucus in terms of preparation."

Hon. Antonio Tinio (ACT TEACHERS Party list Representative):

"We made consultation to them."

Hon. Gary Alejano (MAGDALO Party list Representative):

"We do consultation to our constituents."

3.1.C Is it hard for your Party to formulate such laws/ bills to your constituents?

Hon. Sherwin Tugna (CIBAC Party list Representative):

"It is difficult because you have a lot to consider. It is holistic. You cannot file a bill without repercussion."

Hon. Tom Villarin (AKBAYAN Party list Representative):

"It is not that difficult because we only file the bills based on the concerns of the sector."

Hon. Ron Salo (KABAYAN Party list Representative):

"Yes."

Hon. Gary Alejano (MAGDALO Party list Representative):

"No"

3.1.D Do you receive any support coming from other Parties or other legislators about your proposed laws/bills?

Hon. Sherwin Tugna (CIBAC Party list Representative):

"That's what you call lobbying. We go around, campaign for our bill and discuss to our constituents what we want. What we do is beneficial, especially during election because we establish our political platforms."

Hon. Tom Villarin (AKBAYAN Party list Representative):

"Yes, in terms of legislation you get other representatives to co-sponsor of your bill, so AKBAYAN, belonging to minority, automatic we have six co-sponsors. If you get a lot of co-sponsors on your bill, the bigger chances that it will be approved."

Hon. Antonio Tinio (ACT TEACHERS Party list Representative):

"Well yes, of course. It is important to disseminate the bill to your constituents in order for it to be approved, at least the majority."

Hon. Carlos Isagani Zarate (BAYAN MUNA Party list Representative):

"First and foremost, the MAKABAYAN block, our members include BAYANMUNA, GABRIELA, ANAKPAWIS, ACT TEACHERS and KA-BATAAN Party list. We represent the Party list in Congress. We also have other parties that are not in the Congress like PISTON. All five of us are helping each other with our bills. Other Party list like SSS also helps us because we explain to them the importance of our bill."

Hon. Gary Alejano (MAGDALO Party list Representative):

"Yes, we have a lot of co-authors on the bills that we passed."

> 3.1.E What do you think are the reasons why few members of the Congress support your proposed bills/ laws and why they did not?

Hon. Sherwin Tugna (CIBAC Party list Representative):

"Well of course they have different interests and values. They also represent their own respective sectors. If their sector is in favor of the proposal of their representatives, then they will be in favor of that."

Hon. Tom Villarin (AKBAYAN Party list Representative):

"AKBAYAN's bills are more on national application, so a lot of district congressmen support our bill. The ones who resist are landlords and representatives with vested interest."

Hon. Carlos Isagani Zarate (BAYAN MUNA Party list Representative):

"Some bills are being supported because it is popular or attracts media attention. It is very political."

Discussion:

As the researchers analyze, most Party list began their preparation before the election in their Party Congress, in which they present their main agenda and plan for the duration of their term in Congress. All Party list first conduct a research before they file their bills and went to the different towns or provinces to talk to their constituents to make consultations.

In the aspects of support coming from legislators, most legislators lobby in Congress to ask favors or simply influence other representatives to get their bills approved. However, according to the members of minority group, the co-workers in minority automatically support or co-sponsor the bills that they file.

As confirmed by the Party list representatives, membership in the House is important. If you are part of majority or minority, it affects the passage of your bill and it also has a great impact on support from other legislators.

Challenges Encountered

4. What are the challenges encountered by the Party list Representatives in the course of the delivery of their advocacies, functions and involvement?

4.1 Are there any challenges or problems that your Party experienced?

4.1.A Can you elaborate these specific challenges?

Hon. Sherwin Tugna (CIBAC Party list Representative):

"Well yes, in reality since our advocate is anti-corruption, we have a lot of hurdles. Take for example in city halls, transactions are difficult because of fixers and red tape."

Hon. Tom Villarin (AKBAYAN Party list Representative):

"In democracy, we will encounter opposing views. Us in AKBAYAN, we encourage a healthy debate. Whoever had the soundest view or proposal, he/she will get the full support."

Hon. Ron Salo (KABAYAN Party list Representative):

"The biggest challenge we faced is with Harry Roque. He is my professor in UP College of Law. I was one of his favorite students. I am also one of his friends. I became his co-faculty and even became one of the principal sponsors in my wedding. So that is the main reason how he entered KABAYAN Party list because I was the founder and the chairman. When he entered, people felt a feeling of dominance. He still treats me as one of his students. So we had a concern and it became an issue to the members of the board

because he acts alone and thought what he proposed should be done. He doesn't want to listen to the members of the board. That doesn't how Party list work, in my case we also have a consultation with the members of the board in order to have a decision of the party, not by the person."

Hon. Antonio Tinio (ACT TEACHERS Party list Representative):

"Our main problem is logistics because we campaign nationwide. Our financial resources are very limited. We rely mostly on volunteer work of our members."

Hon. Carlos Isagani Zarate (BAYAN MUNA Party list Representative):

"I think the main problem now is how to strengthen the law by amending in order to strengthen and uphold the objectives mandated by the Constitution about the Party list system."

Hon. Gary Alejano (MAGDALO Party list Representative):

"During the Arroyo Administration, we were denied of accreditation because we are still in jail and they fear that we will just recruit blind followers and destabilize the government. When you apply for accreditation in ComElec, you join the mainstream media; you are allying yourself to be part of government. So the challenge then was low morale and credibility in politics. Second we do not have networks because we are incarcerated and cannot campaign."

> 4.1.B What are the ways or steps you did to solve the challenges of your Party?

Hon. Sherwin Tugna (CIBAC Party list Representative):

"We have discussions within the party to talk about important issues."

Hon. Tom Villarin (AKBAYAN Party list Representative):

"Through discussion, debates and transparency"

Hon. Ron Salo (KABAYAN Party list Representative):

"We have a consultation with the members of the board so decision of the

party, not by the person."

Hon. Antonio Tinio (ACT TEACHERS Party list Representative):

"We discuss the issues within the organization."

Hon. Carlos Isagani Zarate (BAYAN MUNA Party list Representative):

"There are always challenges within the organization, but it is very menial. The main problem is how to change the society. For us the problem is three-fold: foreign intervention on political, social and economic issues, feudal relations and bureaucrat capitalism where the government is used as a business. As long as this problems are present I think our society will be more irrelevant. Change will happen with complete and radical reforms."

Hon. Gary Alejano (MAGDALO Party list Representative):

"We talk about issues in Executive committee. We have the management so whatever our decision is."

Discussion:

Many of those challenges encountered by the Party list representatives pertain to the advocacies inside the Congress such as to the passage of bills for the sectors they represent as part of their main duties of legislation and the opposing views of their party members against their stand on issues. Second challenge they point out is lack of political machinery or resources like money, which is a known fact that election is expensive.

5

SUMMARY OF FINDINGS, CONCLUSIONS, AND RECOMMENDATIONS

This chapter presents the summary of findings, conclusions and the recommendations. The study was conducted by the researcher to explore and explain the Party list system through its advocacies, functions and program involvement. It also aims the readers to gain deeper understanding about Party list System.

Summary of Findings

Based from the previous discussion of the results, the following are then summarized:

Political Representation

Four (4) of the respondents Party list represent multi-sectoral sectors in the Congress while only two (2) Party list represent marginalized sectors which are for teachers and retired police and military officers. Also, majority of Party list representatives, prior to their election, are members of the sectors they represent.

Advocacies of the Party List

These Party list groups primarily aim to represent those in the marginalized/ unprivileged sectors of the society in legislative and decision-making process in the Congress. Through these groups, they serve as faces and voices of the different sectors in the country who cannot represent or speak for their rights and privileges.

Functions of the Party List

The function of the Party list groups in the society is to legislate/propose laws and bills in the Congress wherein it is anchored to the beliefs and desire of their chosen marginalized/unprivileged sectors. Also, their function is to make policy for the betterment of the lives of their constituents and to promote equality over everyone's differences.

Party List Program Involvement

However, two among six of them (KABAYAN and CIBAC Party list) only offers scholarships and livelihood programs for their members. Although it's not their main function, they're just doing it for the sake of the welfare and development in the lives of their constituents.

Preparation, Planning and Analyzing

Most of the selected Party lists interviewed by the researchers analyze first the situation of their constituents before drafting or proposing certain bills/ laws in the Congress. Well of course, by means of conducting surveys or through one-on-one/personal encounter of the selected representatives, they have now the ideas to plan and prepare for what will be the beneficial and good, not only to their chosen sector/s, but also to the whole Filipino people. The preparations of these selected Party lists aren't that easy. In fact, they need thorough and extensive researches before they propose such laws/ bills. They need to balance the needs or interests of their constituents to the needs of the majority.

Challenges Encountered

According to the data gathered by the researchers, one the common problem that each of the Party list in the Congress is currently facing is the vested interests of their colleagues. That is why some of the bills that they filed have no progress. Furthermore, one of the representatives said that needs in financial support is one of their biggest challenges, since the pork barrel system in the country was already abolished. The budget allocated to them were not that enough to cater the money needed for their programs like scholarship grants, livelihood programs and many other activities, so they decided to remove these programs and focus in proposing/legislating bills.

In addition, having insufficient number of volunteers is also one of their challenges. Even though they have different chapters all over the country, it's hard for them to recruit members, which are very much willing to give their support, time and effort for the betterment of their Party and for their constituents.

Conclusions

From the foregoing findings, the researchers have determined the following conclusions:

1. Majority of the selected Party lists interviewed by the researchers are multi-sectoral rather than marginalized Party lists. In fact, out of six Party lists, four of them were came from multi-sectoral (Bayan Muna, AKBAYAN, KABAYAN, and CIBAC) which means they represent various and different marginalized sectors in the society such as urban poor, women, youth, farmers, indigenous people, fisher folks and the workers. On the other hand, the remaining two Party lists (ACT Teachers and Magdalo Para sa Pilipino Party list) are from marginalized sectors in which they want to represent only one and specific sector in the society.

2. In terms of their advocacies, all of Party lists aim to have a proper representation in the Congress, most especially in legislative or decision- making process. They want to promote equality to everyone regardless of what age, economic status, gender and race you have. Moreover, these six selected Party lists in the Congress also advocates transparency and accountability in public officials and fight against graft and corruption.

3. Next, their main function is to legislate and propose bills which will benefit not only their constituents but also for the general welfare. Also, they are the voices and faces of those in the marginalized/unprivileged sectors of the society that cannot speak or represent themselves in the Congress.

4. One of the challenges that the Party list groups is currently facing is the vested interest or the selfish motives of their co-legislators in the Congress. Some of them will not support and give their approval to one's bills if it transgresses or unfavorable to their self-interest. They are willing to criticize and make the process of one's proposed bills sluggish or slow for it not to be passed in the Congress.

Another challenge for them is the vested interest coming from some of their members inside the Party and from their co-lawmakers. Some of them are willing to pull one another just to serve their personal interest and purpose.

Furthermore, lack of financial support is also their biggest challenge most especially when the election in Party list groups is about to come. They don't have enough money to support their election campaign materials that is why they need to triple their work.

Recommendations

From the foregoing conclusions, the researchers come up with the following recommendations:

1. The government should amend the R.A No. 7941 or the "Party list System Act of 1991" wherein it includes the qualifications, duties and responsibilities of those aspiring Party list candidates in the Country. Also, they should include the consequences or punishments if such elected Party list group cannot perform their advocacies, functions and program involvement in the Congress.

2. The government must strengthen the implementation of the bills pertaining to Party list system so that abusing privileges and power of such government officials may be avoided. It also serves as a ticket towards equality and true representation in the country.

3. The Filipino people need to have knowledge or they should be well-educated enough about the Party list system in the Philippines and how it works in Congress. They must learn the following restrictions or the rules and regulations in selecting or choosing the best Party list group that will represent them in legislative or decision-making processes. Also, the Filipinos should be taught about the legal manners and procedures in election and participation and how to practice our rights as Filipino citizens.

BIBLIOGRAPHY

Journals/Articles

Aceron, J. (2010). *It's the Non-System, Stupid! Explaining 'Mal-development' of Parties in the Philippines.* from Reforming the Philippine Political Party System ideas and initiatives, debates and dynamics, published by: Friedrich Ebert Stiftung

Barasa, V. (2011). *Discussing Substantive Representation with Female MPs in Kenya.*

Gutierrez III, I. (2010). *The Judicially Legislated Concept of Marginalization and the Death of Proportional Representation: The Party List System after Banat and Ang Bagong Bayani, 84 PHIL. L.J. 606.* from Philippine Law Journal.

Lambert, C and Lambert, V.(2012). *Qualitative Descriptive Research: An Acceptable Design.*

Rehfeld, A. (2011). *The Concepts of Representation.* Retrieved August 2011 from *American Political Science Review.*

Santos, S. Jr. (1997). *The Philippines Tries the Party List System (A Progressive Perspective).*

Valli, L. (2012). *Spoken Stories.*

Electronic Sources

Antiquerra, J.R and Mangilit, R. F. (2010). *Revisiting the Party List System.* Retrieved July 1, 2010 http://cmfr-phil.org/mediaandelections/2010-elections/sidebar-revisiting- the-party-list-system-and-what-the-media-missed/

Buenagua, J.M (2010). *The Philippine Party List System in the 14th Congress: A Study.* Retrieved March 5, 2010 https://www.scribd.com/document/30682757/The-Party-List-System

COMELEC Resolution No. 3307. http://www.chanrobles.com/comelecresolutiono3307a.htm#.W6EJ6J-tTIU

De Asis, C., Flores, C. & Navarro, T. (2010) *Party List Groups and its Role in Society.* Retrieved October, 16, 2010 https://quillonline.wordpress.com/2010/10/16/

Grande, G. (2016). *Report Card: Would you vote for these party list groups again?.* Retrieved February 11, 2016 http://news.abs-cbn.com/halalan2016/focus/02/11/16/

Grande, G. (2016). *For these party list groups, it's mission possible.* Retrieved February 16, 2016 http://news.abs-cbn.com/halalan2016/focus/02/16/16/

Llaneta, C.A. (2013). *Political Power and the Party List System.* Retrieved April 30, 2013 http://www.up.edu.ph/political-power-and-the-party-list-system/

Marquez, D. (2016). *Understanding the Party List System of the Philippines.* http://filamstar.net/rp-news/3159-understanding-the-party-list-system-of- the-philippines.html

Panganiban, CJ A. (2010). *The Party list System, Philippine Style Presenting better solutions, or hatching new problems?.* Retrieved November 18, 2010 https://www.google.com.ph/amp/s/cjpanganiban.com/2010/11/18/

Remollino, A.M (2007). *Reviewing the Party List Law and the 2004 Election.* Retrieved April 7, 2007 http://www.bulatlat.com/news/7-9/7-9-pl1.htm

Republic Act 7941 of 1995

Tan, O. F. (2010). *Party list systems' dirty secret.* Retrieved from https://www.google.com.ph/amp/opinion.inquirer.net/38998/

www.congress.gov.ph

www.makabayan.net

https://akbayan.org.ph www.magdalo.org

APPENDICES

APPENDIX A
Republic Act No. 7941

AN ACT PROVIDING FOR THE ELECTION OF PARTY LIST REPRESENTATIVES THROUGH THE PARTY LIST SYSTEM

Be it enacted by the Senate and House of Representatives of the Philippines in Congress assembled:

Section 1. *Title.* - This Act shall be known as the "Party List System Act".

Section 2. *Declaration of Policy.* - The State shall promote proportional representation in the election of representatives to the House of Representatives through a party list system of registered national, regional and sectoral parties or organizations or coalitions thereof, which will enable Filipino citizens belonging to the marginalized and underrepresented sectors, organizations and parties, and who lack well-defined political constituencies but who could contribute to the formulation and enactment of appropriate legislation that will benefit the nation as a whole, to become members of the House of Representatives. Towards this end, the State shall develop and guarantee a full, free and open party system in order to attain the broadest possible representation of party, sectoral or group interests in the House of Representatives by enhancing their chances to compete for and win seats in the legislature, and shall provide the simplest scheme possible.

Section 3. *Definition of Terms.* (The party list system is a mechanism of proportional representation in the election of representatives to the House of Representatives from national, regional and sectoral parties or organizations or coalitions thereof registered with the Commission on Elections (COMELEC). Component parties or organizations of a coalition may participate independently provid ed the coalition of which they form part does not participate in the party-list system.

- A party means either a political party or a sectoral party or a coalition of parties.
- A political party refers to an organized group of citizens advocating an ideology or platform, principles and policies for the general conduct of government and which, as the most immediate means of securing their adoption, regularly nominates and supports certain of its leaders and members as candidates for public office.
- It is a national party when its constituency is spread over the geographical territory of at least a majority of the regions.
- It is a regional party when its constituency is spread over the geo-

graphical territory of at least a majority of the cities and provinces comprising the region.

- A sectoral party refers to an organized group of citizens belonging to any of the sectors enumerated in Section 5 hereof whose principal advocacy pertains to the special interests and concerns of their sector.
- A sectoral organization refers to a group of citizens or a coalition of groups of citizens who share similar physical attributes or characteristics, employment, interest or concerns.
- A coalition refers to an aggrupation of duly registered national, regional, sectoral parties or organizations for political and/or election purposes.

Section 4. *Manifestation to Participate in the Party List System.* - Any party, organization, or coalition already registered with the Commission need not register anew. However, such party, organization or coalition shall file with the Commission, not later than ninety (90) days before the election, a manifestation of its desire to participate in the party-list system.

Section 5. *Registration.* - Any organized group of persons may register as a party, organization or coalition for purposes of the party-list system by filing with the COMELEC not later than ninety (90) days before the election a petition verified by its president or secretary stating its desire to participate in the party- list system as a national, regional or sectoral party or organization or a coalition of such parties or organizations, attaching thereto its constitution, by-laws, platform or program of government, list of officers, coalition agreement and other relevant information as the COMELEC may require: provided, that the sectors shall include labor, peasant, fisherfolk, urban poor, indigenous cultural communities, elderly, handicapped, women, youth, veterans, overseas workers, and professionals.

The COMELEC shall publish the petition in at least two (2) national newspapers of general circulation.

The COMELEC shall, after due notice and hearing, resolve the petition within fifteen (15) days from the date it was submitted for decision but in no case not later than sixty (60) days before election.

Section 6. *Removal and/or Cancellation of Registration.* - The COMELEC may motu proprio or upon verified complaint of any interested party, remove or cancel, after due notice and hearing, the registration of any national, regional or sectoral party, organization or coalition on any of the following grounds:

- It is a religious sect or denomination, organization or association organized for religious purposes;

- It advocates violence or unlawful means to seek its goal;
- It is a foreign party or organization;
- It is receiving support from any foreign government, foreign political party, foundation, organization, whether directly or through any of its officers or members or indirectly through third parties for partisan election purposes;
- It violates or fails to comply with laws, rules or regulations relating to elections;
- It declares untruthful statements in its petition;
- It has ceased to exist for at least one (1) year; or
- It fails to participate in the last two (2) preceding elections or fails to obtain at least two percentum (2%) of the votes cast under the party-list system in the two (2) preceding elections for the constituency in which it has registered.

Section 7. *Certified List of Registered Parties.* - The COMELEC shall, not later than sixty (60) days before election, prepare a certified list of national, regional, or sectoral parties, organizations or coalitions which have applied or who have manifested their desire to participate under the party list system and distribute copies thereof to all precincts for posting in the polling places on election day. The names of the party list nominees shall not be shown on the certified list.

Section 8. *Nominations of Party list Representatives.* - Each registered party, organization or coalition shall submit to the COMELEC not later than forty-five (45) days before the election a list of names, not less than five (5) from which party list representatives shall be chosen in case it obtains the required number of votes.

A person may be nominated in one (1) list only. Only persons who have given their consent in writing may be named in the list. The list shall not include any candidate for any elective office or person who has lost his bid for an elective office in the immediately preceding election. No change of names or alteration of the order of nominees shall be allowed after the same shall have been submitted to the COMELEC except in cases where the nominee dies, or withdraws in writing, his nomination, becomes incapacitated in which case the name of the substitutes nominee shall be placed last in the list. Incumbent sectoral representatives in the House of Representatives who are nominated in the party-list system shall not be considered resigned.

Section 9. *Qualification of Party list Nominees.* - No person shall be nominated as party-list representative unless he is a natural born citizen of the

Philippines, a registered voter, a resident of the Philippines for a period of not less than one (1) year immediately preceding the day of the election, able to read and write, bona fide member of the party or organization which he seeks to represent for at least ninety (90) days preceding the day of the election, and is at least twenty-five (25) years of age on the day of the election.

In case of a nominee of the youth sector, he must at least be twenty-five (25) but not more than thirty (30) years of age on the day of the election. Any youth sectoral representative who attains the age of thirty during his term shall be allowed to continue until the expiration of his term.

Section 10. *Manner of Voting.* - Every voter shall be entitled to two (2) votes. The first is a vote for candidate for member of the House of Representatives in his legislative district, and the second, a vote for the party, organization, or coalition he wants represented in the House of Representatives: provided, that a vote cast for a party, sectoral organization, or coalition not entitled to be voted for shall not be counted: provided, finally that the first election under the party list system shall be held in May 1998.

The COMELEC shall undertake the necessary information campaign for purposes of educating the electorate on the matter of the party-list system.

Section 11. *Number of Party list Representatives.* - The party list representatives shall constitute twenty percentum (20%) of the total number of the members of the House of Representatives including those under the party list.

For purposes of the May 1998 elections, the first five (5) major political parties on the basis of party representation in the House of Representatives at the start of the Tenth Congress of the Philippines shall not be entitled to participate in the party list system.

In determining the allocation of seats for the second vote, the following procedure shall be observed: The parties, organizations, and coalitions shall be ranked from the highest to the lowest based on the number of votes garnered during the elections.

The parties, organizations, and coalitions receiving at least two percent (2%) of the total votes cast for the party-list system shall be entitled to one seat each: provided, that those garnering more than two percent (2%) of the votes shall be entitled to additional seats in proportion to their total number of votes: provided, finally, that each party, organization, or coalition shall be entitled to not more than three (3) seats.

Section 12. *Procedure in Allocating Seats for Party list Representatives.* - The COMELEC shall tally all the votes for the parties, organizations, or coalitions on a nationwide basis, rank them according to the number of votes received and allocate party-list representatives proportionately according to the percentage of votes obtained by each party, organization, or coalition as against the total nationwide votes cast for the party list system.

Section 13. *How Party list Representatives are Chosen.* (C Party list representatives shall be proclaimed by the COMELEC based on the list of names submitted by the respective parties, organizations, or coalitions to the COMELEC according to their ranking in the said list.

Section 14. *Term of Office.* (C Party list representatives shall be elected for a term of three (3) years which shall begin, unless otherwise provided by law, at noon on the thirtieth day of June next following their election. No party list representatives shall serve for more than three (3) consecutive terms. Voluntary renunciation of the office for any length of time shall not be considered as an interruption in the continuity of his service for the full term for which he was elected.

Section 15. *Change of Affiliation Effect.* - Any elected part -list representative who changes his political party or sectoral affiliation during his term of office shall forfeit his seat: provided, that if he changes his political party or sectoral affiliation within six (6) months before an election, he shall not be eligible for nomination as party list representative under his new party or organization. Section 16. Vacancy. - In case of vacancy in seats reserved for party list representatives, the vacancy shall be automatically filled by the next representative from the list of nominees in the order submitted to the COMELEC by the same party, organization, or coalition, who shall serve for the unexpired term. If the list is exhausted, the party, organization, or coalition concerned shall submit additional nominees.

Section 17. *Rights of Party list Representatives.* (C Party list representatives shall be entitled to the same salaries and emoluments as regular members of the House of Representatives. Section 18. Rules and Regulations. - The COMELEC shall promulgate the necessary rules and regulations as may be necessary to carry out the purpose of this Act.

Section 19. *Appropriations.* - The amount necessary for the implementation of this Act shall be provided in the regular appropriations for the Commission on Elections starting fiscal year 1996 under the General Appropriations Act. Starting 1995, the COMELEC is hereby authorized to utilize savings and other available funds for purposes of its information campaign on the party list system.

Section 20. *Separability Clause.* - If any part of this Act is held invalid or unconstitutional, the other parts or provisions thereof shall remain valid and effective.

Section 21. *Repealing Clause.* - All laws, decrees, executive orders, rules and regulations, or parts thereof, inconsistent with the provisions of this Act are hereby repealed.

APPENDIX B
Letter of request

Republic of the Philippines
HOUSE OF REPRESENTATIVES

CARLOS ISAGANI T. ZARATE
REPRESENTATIVE, BAYAN MUNA PARTY-LIST

417 North Wing, House of Representatives, Batasan Hills, Quezon City 1126

...ublic of the Philippines
...HNOLOGICAL UNIVERSITY
...ge of Arts and Sciences
...NT OF POLITICAL SCIENCE

HON. CARLOS ISAGANI ZARATE
PARTYLIST REPRESENTATIVE
BAYAN MUNA PARTYLIST

Dear Hon. Zarate,

We, the undersigned, are fourth year students of Rizal Technological University pursuing a degree in Bachelor of Arts in Political Science and are currently enrolled in Thesis Writing 2 undertaking a research titled "**Party list System: Its Advocacies, Functions and Programs Involvement**".
As part of our thesis subject, we would like to conduct an interview with you on the above topic.

We are looking forward that our request would merit your positive response.

Thank you and more power.

Sincerely,

Jhon Vincent M. Avelino

Angelito Y. Aviles

Alexis V. Belarmino

Marvin M. Magtabog

Nell Adrian C. Pastrana

Noted by;

Mr. Michael M. Mesinas
Thesis Adviser

Republic of the Philippines
RIZAL TECHNOLOGICAL UNIVERSITY
College of Arts and Sciences
DEPARTMENT OF POLITICAL SCIENCE

HON, TOM VILLARIN
PARTYLIST REPRESENTATIVE
AKBAYAN CITIZENS' ACTION PARTY

Dear Hon. Villarin,

We, the undersigned, are fourth year students of Rizal Technological University pursuing a degree in Bachelor of Arts in Political Science and are currently enrolled in Thesis Writing 2 undertaking a research titled **"Party list System: Its Advocacies, Functions and Programs Involvement ".**
As part of our thesis subject, we would like to conduct an interview with you on the above topic.

We are looking forward that our request would merit your positive response.

Thank you and more power.

Sincerely,

Jhon Vincent M. Avelino

Angelito Y. Aviles

Alexis V. Belarmino

Marvin M. Magtabog

Neil Adrian C. Pastrana

Noted by:

Mr.Michael M. Mesinas
Thesis Adviser

Republic of the Philippines
RIZAL TECHNOLOGICAL UNIVERSITY
College of Arts and Sciences
DEPARTMENT OF POLITICAL SCIENCE

HON. SHERWIN TUGNA
PARTYLIST REPRESENTATIVE
CIBAC PARTYLIST

Dear Hon.Tugna,

We, the undersigned, are fourth year students of Rizal Technological University pursuing a degree in Bachelor of Arts in Political Science and are currently enrolled in Thesis Writing 2 undertaking a research entitled **"Party list System: Its Advocacies, Functions and Programs Involvement "**. As part of our thesis subject, we would like to conduct an interview with you on the above topic.

We are looking forward that our request would merit your positive response.

Thank you and more power.

Sincerely,

Jhon Vincent M. Avelino

Angelito Y. Aviles

Alexis V. Belarmino

Marvin M. Magtabog

Neil Adrian C. Pastrana

Noted by:

Mr. Michael M. Mesinas
Thesis Adviser

Rep. Antonio L. Tinio
Party-List Representative, ACT TEACHERS
Chairman, House Committee on Public Information

Room 513 South Wing, House of Representatives, Batasan Hills,
Quezon City, Philippines 1126 • Mobile: +63920 0220817
Phone/Fax: +632-931.61.93 • Email: rep.antonio.tinio@gmail.com

...ublic of the Philippines
...HNOLOGICAL UNIVERSITY
...ege of Arts and Sciences
...NT OF POLITICAL SCIENCE

HON. ANTONIO TINIO
PARTYLIST REPRESENTATIVE
ACT TEACHERS

Dear Hon. Tinio,

We, the undersigned, are fourth year students of Rizal Technological University pursuing a degree in Bachelor of Arts in Political Science and are currently enrolled in Thesis Writing 2 undertaking a research titled **"Party list System: Its Advocacies, Functions and Programs Involvement "**.

As part of our thesis subject, we would like to conduct an interview with you on the above topic. We are looking forward that our request would merit your positive response.

Thank you and more power.

Sincerely,
Jhon Vincent M. Aveling
Angelito Y. Aviles
Alexis V. Belarmino
Marvin M. Magtabog
Neil Adrian C. Pastrana

Noted by:

Mr. Michael M. Mesinas
Thesis Adviser

Republic of the Philippines
RIZAL TECHNOLOGICAL UNIVERSITY
College of Arts and Sciences
DEPARTMENT OF POLITICAL SCIENCE

HON. GARY ALEJANO
PARTYLIST REPRESENTATIVE
MAGDALO

Dear Hon.Alejano,
We, the undersigned, are fourth year students of Rizal Technological University pursuing a degree in Bachelor of Arts in Political Science and are currently enrolled in Thesis Writing 2 undertaking a research titled "**Party list System: Its Advocacies, Functions and Programs Involvement** ".
As part of our thesis subject, we would like to conduct an interview with you on the above topic. We are looking forward that our request would merit your positive response.
Thank you and more power.

Sincerely,
Jhon Vincent M. Avelino
Angelito Y. Aviles
Alexis V. Belarmino
Marvin M. Magtabog
Neil Adrian C. Pastrana

Noted by:

Mr. Michael M. Mesinas
Thesis Adviser

Received by: Rep. Gary C. Alejano
MAGDALO
29 Nov 2017

APPENDIX C
Interview Sheet Questionnaires

1. What is the Political representation of your Party?

A. To be specific, what sector/s you're Party representing?

B. Do you belong to the group that you representing?

C. As you represent this sector/s, what is your priority?

D. When did you realize that you want to represent this kind of sector/s in the Congress?

  D.1 What is the first thing you do after your Party earned seat/s in the Congress? And how do you feel about that?

2. What is your Party's main advocacy?

A. If _____ is your main advocacy, are there any advocacies for other sector/s you represent? Can you enumerate them?

B. What are the steps your Party is taking to accomplish those advocacies you mentioned above?

3. How does your Party works in the Congress?

A. What is the role of your Party inside or outside of the Congress?

B. Aside from creating or proposing bills/ laws for the sector/s, what else are the other things that your Party is doing to help your constituents/ members to be more productive and well-function to our community?

C. Do you think your members/ constituents appreciate the efforts and presence of your Party? Do you have any data that will support your claim? Can we have a copy of it?

D. Are there any instances that your Party failed to do for at least once, your Party's functions most especially in proposing/ legislating certain laws in the Congress?

E. Why do you think you fail?

4. What is the status of your current bill? Are there any support coming from other legislators?

A. Is there any pending bill your Party filed/ proposed in the Congress to support your Party's program involvement?

B. What appropriate policy would you propose in order to achieve reform in our current Party list System?

B.1 We know that we have 4 inviolable parameters in electing Party list members: 2% threshold, three seat-limit chair, 20% allocation and proportional representation. If you have given a chance to amend or reform any of the 4 inviolable parameters, what would it be? Why?

C. Do you have internal rules and regulations that should be followed by your Party members?

C.1 Are you that type of leader who's very strict in implementing your Party's rules and regulations?

C.2 How do you give punishments to those who violates your Party's rules and regulations and do you give them such considerations/ second chances for them to correct their mistakes?

5. What are the preparations that your Party is doing in proposing bills/ laws and how prepared is your Party for the possible outcomes whether it's negative or positive?

A. How does your Party formulate the bills/ laws that will be proposed in the Congress? Did you just base it in your own perception or to the beneficiary constituents?

B. What method of referral you made? Did you just present it to them with discussion or you just conducted a survey first before you draft it?

C. Is it hard for your Party to formulate such laws/ bills to your constituents?

D. Do you receive any support coming from other Parties or other legislators about your proposed laws/ bills?

E. What do you think are the reasons why few members of the Congress support your proposed bills/ laws and why they did not?

6. Are there any challenges or problems that your Party experienced?

A. Can you elaborate these specific challenges?

B. What are the ways or steps you did to solve the challenges of your Party?

Congressman Carlos Isagani Zarate of BAYAN MUNA Party list (August 30, 2017)

I: What is the Political representation of your Party?

Cong. Zarate: Well ang BAYANMUNA is a multisectoral political party, wala syang particular na sector na nirerepresent, dahil under R.A 7941 or the partylist system law pwede namang ang kabahagi ng party list system ay pwedeng sectoral party or sectoral organization or political party, BAYANMUNA again is not a just sectoral it's a multisectoral party so lahat dala-dala nya yung samu't saring issues confronting our marginalized sectors, from the peasants to the marginalized workers, informal settlers, urban poor even our marginalize professionals government employees, middle class students, indigenous people or moro people for as lng us they belong to our marginalized sector so ayun yung dala-dala ng BAYANMUNA so our name in itself defined who we are BAYANMUNA bago ang sarili, BAYANMUNA bago ang dayuhan, BAYUNMUNA higit sa lahat hindi ang iilan.

I: To be specific, what sector/s you're Party representing?

Cong. Zarate: Wala kaming specific na nirerepresent lahat ng mga sector na mahihirap or marginalized descent franchise sector halimbawa ang mga persons with disablties mga senior citizens na kabahagi na din ng aming mga advocacies, urban poor nirerepresent namin silang lahat dito sa loob at labas ng kongreso.

I: Do you belong to the group that you representing?

Cong. Zarate: Of course you cannot effectively represent or pwedeng dalhin ang boses ng marginalized or mahihirap kung hindi ka galing sa kanilang sector mismo kaya satingin ko isang requirment na dapat ang represantasyon ng mga nasa partylist ang kanilang mga kinatawan ay talagang nagmumula sa kanilang sector na nirerepresentahan hindi pepwedeng yung sinasabing na may partylist kayo ng mga security guard or mga tricycle driver, eh hindi ka marunong magdrive ng tricycle or maging isang security guard. later on i explain yan yung isang pamamaraan na pag- standardize ng partylist system.

I: As you represent this sector/s, what is your priority?

Cong. Zarate: Well unang unang dahil multisectoral nga ang bayanmuna syemnpre ang prioritize natin ay halimbawa dito sa loob ng congress, dahil dito ang pangunahing larangan ng pagkilos ng bayanmuna sa parylist, ang pangunahing sinusulong nya yung mga panukalang batas initially una pangunahing batas pangalawa panukalang resolusyon, para sa kagalingan ng ating mga mamamayan ang Pilipinas ay isang agricultural na bansa, walo sa bawat sampung masasaka ay walang lupang sinasaka hanggan ngayon hindi nila pagaari yung lupang kanilang ipinagsasaka, despite of so many agrarian reform laws that passed in the past administrations hannggan ngayon na sumusukling tugunan yung problema ng kawalang ng lupa ng mga magsasaka bakit pangunahin problema yun? Dahil halos 75% to 80% of our population nakadepende sa pagsaka ng lupa kaya kahit na sabihin mo na "Ah maramin naman kaming ano eh, andito na kami sa syudad."Pero kalakhan ng ating populasyon ay nandoon parin sa pagsasaka at kung yun ang realidad sa ating bansa dapat yun ang pangunahing tugunan natin kaya ang aming priority ay halimbawa ang pagsulong ng isang tunay na batas para sa repormang agraryo yung tinatawag na Comprehensive Agrarian Reform Bill andyan din ang batas para sa tinatawag na pangaganalaga sa ating likas na yaman yung People's Mining Bill na gusto nating baguhin ang orientation ng pagmimina sa ating bayan na sa halip kagaya ng kasalukuyan ang orientation ng pagmimina sating bayan ay highly instructive, export oriented and foreign capitalist driven gusto nating baliktarin yan na dapat ang mining sa ating bayan ay makatulong para sa pambansang industrilasyon so kung magmimina tayo ng ating mga likas yaman hindi to pang export dapat gamitin ito linangin ito para makatulong ito sa ating industrilasyon at kung ganun ang mangyayari it will spare development will create jobs, employment na sa halip ngayon na ang ating raw materials or natural resousrcer ay ini-export its raw form walang value added pagbalik sa atin dito ini-import natin finish product, sequel lang yan ang isang masaklap na katotohanan na even up to now in the age of advance information technology, internet, smartphones na kahit na pako ini-import natin kahit na pardible ini- import natin sa ibang countries well in fact all the raw material ay galing satin, ang ibig ba sabihin nyan bobo ang mga Pilipino na hindi pwede gumawa ng pako at gumawa ng pardible? Hindi, dahil sa katunayan maraming mga imbentor mga inhinyero lahat ng propesyonal sa ibang bansa pinakikinabangan ng ibang bansa, so balik dun sa tanong ano yung priority yun ang pangunahing sinusulong naming dito magmula ng pumasok ang bayanmuna sa kongreso noong 2001 isang makabuluhang tunay na repormang agraryo batas mula sa pag-o-orient ng peoples mining bill in fact ang mga ka-akibat nyan yung mga batas para sa pambansang industrilasyon dahil yun ang satingin naming ang tumbungan na tunay na development na paglago ng ating bansa, hindi itong kasalukuyan o noon pa man hanggang ngayon patuloy na programa ng pamahalaan na export oriented lang tayo we are exporting all our natural resources even our number one resource, and what is that? Tao, ang number one export naman natin is human resources we prouduce thousands and thousands of graduates every year.

I: When did you realize that you want to represent this kind of sector/s in the Congress?

Cong. Zarate: Well personally that realization hindi ko naman pangarap pumasok ng kongreso at maging kongresista pero naging kabahagi na ako ng BAYANMUNA noong since 2001. Noong 1999 even sakanyang initial states of organizing in 1998 sa Mindanao that time I was already practicing lawyer a human rights lawyer so ang first na ano ko muna sa BAYANMUNA is legal- council ng BAYANMUNA sa Mindanao eventually I was nominated in 2012 as second nominee of the party pinalad na nakadalawnag seats ang BAYANMUNA kaya nakapasok ako.

I: What is the first thing you do after your Party earned seat/s in the Congress? And how do you feel about that?

Cong. Zarate: Noong pumasok ako sa kongreso noong 2013 even the prior of that ang isang pinaka-mainit na issue noon ay ang pagsabog ng pork barrel if we can recall the February of that year 2013 nag away yung mag-tita na si benhur luy at si janet napoles at nagging campaign issue yung pork barrel that's why when I join the 16th congress the first house bill that I signed was the bill that abolish the pork barrel system, in fact as a new fight of legislator that time I was caught by some of senior legislator here some are jokingly some are seriously, talagang nagalit sila, sabi nila kabago-bago mo sa kongreso pinapalabas nila ume-epal ka kaagad ipapa-abolish daw ang prok barrel. May nagsabi na isa na "Kababata mo pa at siguro kailangan mo muna tikman ang pork barrel para malaman mo kung ano ang lasa ng pork."Ang sabi ko naman "Sorry po dahil vegetarian ako kaya ayoko ng pork."Seriously napakalaking laban nyun as a new lesgilator ang BAYANMUNA at ang aming block na MAKABAYAN talagang nanawagan na i-abolish ang Pork Barrel dahil na satingin nga naming na tatlong mayor na problema ng bansa ay isa dyan ang usaping Pork Barrel yan yung ginagamit na dugtungan ng mga bureaucrats at gawing negosyo ang gobyerno so sa tatlong mayor ng problema natin yung pangingi-alam ng dayuhang ang principal dyan ang America noon at hang-gang ngayon, pangalawa yung na kwento ko na kanina kung bakit kailangan natin ng Agrarian Reform, Feudal na relasyon pa rin sa ating bayan ngayon na noon at ngayon walo pa rin sa bawat sampung magsasaka ang wala paring sinasaka kaya hindi tayo umuunlad, so pangatlo itong ginagawang negosyo itong gobyerno may term kami dyan mga aktibista bureaucrats capitalism ginagawa negosyo ng mga bureacrats they entered the congress they entered the executive all the branches of the Government not to serve the people but to make it as a dugtungan ng kanilang negosyo to protect their economic interest, but worst hindi lang sila bumabalik dito sa kongreso di lang sila pumapasok sa kongreso to protect their economic interest ginagamit pa nila yung pondo ng bayan to advance and protect their economic interest at yan yung pork barrel pera natin yan pero ayan yung ginagamit nila sa kanilang negosyo so yan ang malala so sabi naming noon dapat ng tanggalin ang pork barrel ang sabi nga nila noong 2013 "that's imposibble suntok sa buwan"pero anyway kahit binanatan kami noon dito sa loob pero ok lang dahil minsan din pala nasusuntok ang buwan, Sept of that year SC declared that Pork Barrel system is unconstitutional declared it illegal, kung andito kayo non nasa ganitong pana-hon din kami non nasa budget deliberation nung sumabog yung pork barrel scandal, I can still remember nasa plenary kami nun it was Wednesday, if I'm not mistaken, pero ang lungkot lungkot ng plenaryo, ang layo ng tingin, bakit sila malungkot? Dahil pag wala ng Pork Barrel, iniisip nila *"Paano na kami mabubuhay? paano yung projects naming? paano yung kickbacks?"* and at that time grabe na yung mga sumabog na detalye, unang sumabog ito was I think, meron ding scandal noon it was 1998 or 1999 ata, dito din sa congress about the Pork Barrel, pero ang scandal noon or yung kickbacks noon is nasa 5% to 10%, pero ngayon yung kay "Napoles Pork Barrel Scandal"is 100% na pala wala ng projects na ini-implement kumbaga kickbacks na lang, pagkabigay ng PDAF nila, pinaghatihatian na nila. Actually yung mga pangalan ng reciepi-ents nila is galing na lang sa phone directory ganun kalala ang pork barrel. So ayun yung unang pag-pasok ko sa congress, ang paglaban sa Pork Barrel. And nasundan yun nung mabisto namin na hindi lang ang mambabatas ang may pork barrel, ang pinakamalaking pork barrel na tangang-tanga nya ay nasa presidente ng pilipinas yung DAF. Kaya tinawag naming si Aquino nyun ng "Pork Barrel King"dahil kung ang PDAF that time ay nasa 24 billion every year buo na yun sa senado at kongreso. Ang DAF 757 Billion tangang-tanga ni

Aquino at nilaro nya ang pondo, kaya isa ako sa naging petitioner na umakyat ulit sa Supreme Court kiniwestyon namin yung DAF and nag-argue ako sa Supreme Court para i-declare na unconstituitional ang DAF, we went to the supreme court in September of 2013 and the Supreme Court decided June of 2014 at diniclare nya ang DAF as unconstitutional. So yun yung mga new fight as a new legislator and as my first year in the senate. So paano naming nagawa yun? We join the People's Initiative against Pork (PIP) nanawagan ng initiative, invoking the law and initiative na i-abolish ang pork barrel.

I: What is your Party's main advocacy?

Cong. Zarate: Well siguro ibalik ko ulit muna, well ang advocacy ng BAYAN-MUNA since pumasok ito sa kongreso noong 2001 generally is to advanced yung causes ng mga marginalised sector and kung sabihin nating marginalised sector kalakhan nyan is mga magsasaka, mga workers at yung mga disadvantaged sa society mga urban poor, mga indigenous group so dahil ang congress is an institution taga-graft ng batas dala dala natin yan na advocacies dito sa pagsulong ng mga batas dahil kalakhan na karamihan talaga na batas dito ay talagang, kaya nga sinabi ko na ang congress ay conservative and reactional institution dahil sino ba ang nagcocompose ng congress at kapag nagpasa sila ng batas ano bang batas ang ipapasa nila? So kahit na magconduct ka ng survey sa mga batas dito siguro 99% ay pabor para sa mga naghaharing uri mga landlords kahit na sabihin nila na ano eh may principle kasi sa batas na *"Dura Lex Sed Lex!"* which means *"The law is harsh but it is the law!"* it equalise to all pero ang problema dyan is ang nagpasa nito ang mga miyembro ng oligarchs na mga nahaharing uri, so yung batas na yan nilalagyan nila ng punto yan na makakalabas sila kahit na magsurvey ka ngayon sa mga kulungan ang karamihan sa mga yan ay mahihirap so ayun yun interms of our advocacies so ayun yung papel naming dito sa congress ilatag, i- surface ang mga issue ng mga mamamayan kahit na sabihin pa nila na talo naman kayo by numbers but since 2001 I think the Philippine congress is no longer the same ng pumasok ang mga progressive in our history may mga panapanahon na nakakapasok ang mga progressive sa congress even it is conservative or a reactionary institution but talaga naka- suppress yan but since 2001 up to now andyan yung pag-suppress pa rin in fact ang BAYANMUNA ang pinakamaraming pinatay na miyembro since 2001 among the party list dahil gustong i-suppress dahil magiging boses sya kahit hindi man kami manalo sa legislation hindi man maitulak yan hindi man maging batas yan ay talagang haharangin yan sabi ko nga kanina na kahit yung buong 25% progressive pa yan na sa party list kung

75% naman ang nagrerepresent sa ruling class at sa mga oligarchs ay hindi ka pa rin mananalo pero bakit pumapasok pa rin to bakit nag-e-engage pa rin kami sa congress para i- highlight para i-surface at isa ito para sa mamamayan para malaman ng mamamayan na ito pala yung klase ng trade sa kongreso hindi pala talaga dinadala ang yung usaping trade Tax Reform ang dami dami naming nakausap na kongresista na ayaw nila na sa Tax Reform pero noon botohan ilan lang kami sampu, pito sa MAKABAYAN tatlo sa independent at isa kaming sa super majority, sa death penalty ang daming may ayaw death penalty dahil takot sila sa bishop nila daw nagmagka-botohan ilan lang kaming bumoto against the death penalty so nevertheless kailangan mong I-ano yan para malaman ng mamamayan dahil nga sabi namin eventually darating ang panahon na mananagot ang dapat na mananagot, hindi naman sa habang panahon na ang mamamayang Pilipino ay mag-kikimkim at tatahimik lang yan sabi ko nga ang tunay na pagbabago ay hindi mang-gagaling sa kongreso kundi sa atin ding mga Pilipino at lalo na kayo Malaki ang inyong papel bilang kabataan para imulat din ang kapareho nyong kabataan.

I: How does your Party works in the Congress?

Cong. Zarate: Dito sa 17th congress dahil kabahagi kami ng super majority may mga advantages pero may mga limitations. Advantages in the sense of yung access mo is, for example dahil nasa commitees kami you can talk to the leadership but may mga limitations din, dahil nga nasa super majirty ka yung kaya mong gawin is full blast yun kung minority ka may limitations talga dito. In over-all alam ng mga liderato na tatayo at tatayo kami dito independently kung ano naging tindig ng super majority specially in the advent or satingin naming dito, halimbawa dito sa 17th congress yung mga minority minsan hindi naman bumuboto halos kabahagi lang sila ng majority dahil kung ano ang boto ng majority dun lang din sila bumoboto halimbawa sample noong nakaraang araw nang pinasa ang compress work week for the worker, kung titignan mo parang ang ganda biro mo apat na araw na lang ang trabaho pero pag-atras yun sa pagka-panalo ng mga mang-gagawa na dapat ang trabaho ay walong oras na lang dapat liitan mo ang numero ng pagtrabaho. Kung liitan mo ang number of days ng pagtrabaho ng isang mang-gagawa dapat liitan mo din ang number of hours ng pagtatrabaho ng isang mang-gagawa na walang pagbawas sa kanyang sahod pero dito ang work fixed mo ay magta-trabaho ka naman ng pagkahaba-haba na oras it's more than 8 hours. Sabi nila at least meron kang tatlong araw na pahinga pero bugbog ka naman at wala ka naming dagdag na benepisyo talo ka pa rin. So ayun parang kami lang ata ang bumoto sa MAKABAYAN na nag-"NO"so yun yung mga limititations and eventually dahil sa mga recents developments wala na yung peace talks nasa bingit ng alangin ang peace talks yung mga basis for supporting the administration halimbawa yung peace talk yung mga presence ng mga progressive for the cabinet, ngayong araw na kasalang si Rafael Mariano sa Commission on Appointment ba ka i-reject nanaman siya yung independent foreign policy ni Duterte sabi niya Independent foreign policy pero parang lumalaro-laro lang sa mga hingante America, China, and Russia napaka-delikado nyun and itong mga nangyayaring walang habas na patayan talagang hindi na katanggap-tanggap ito, itong sinasabi nilang war on drugs, make me mistake about it we supported the campaign about laban sa droga dahil napakalala na rin ng problema sa droga pero ang solusyon dito satingin naming ay hindi itong grabing patayan ang pinapatay mo itong mahihirap at ito minsan ay hindi naiintindihan kung bakit ayaw naming nangyayaring patayan na ngayon, lalong lalo na itong patayan kay kean walang kasalanan ang bata pero ang sabi nila nanlaban buti na lang may CCTV kung walang CCTV si Kean ay kabilang sa con-statistic na pinatay dahil adik, courier, pusher. Meron bang kritikal na pagtingin ito? Last august, last year naghain na kami ng resolusyon dito to ivestigate at that time ang namatay ay 1,200 palang guess what last year pa yan we warned the administration if will this not be investigated it will be underline the campaign against drug. Kasi sinusuportahan naming yan e pero not at the point na wala ng judicial process wala ng human rights that is not the serve to a complex problem like drugs dapat tignan ang mga mahihirap lalo na at biktima sila, nauubos na yung mga patayan pero tuloy tuloy parin ang pasok ng shabu sa ating bansa, sino nagpapasok nito? Ang mga mayayaman na may mga connection sa gobyerno na corrupt na official dapat unahin muna sila i-reporma kagaya ng PNP sabi ni Duterte "Corrupt ang PNP"from PO1 to General may mga kasama dyan na drug syndicate. Eh di ayun yung unahin na linisin alam nyo yun, napakadali sakanilang linisan ang mga "Mahihirap"pero kaya ba nila linisin yung mga nasa mga kilalang subdivision na mayayaman? Are you saying na mga adik ay nasa slam area lang? that is the issue, bakit it is amaze na yung can solve this complex problem through military selection any maze and any solution that can be founded in the maze they surely frame tinuro sa atin yan ng ating kasaysayan na ganyang klaseng pamamaraan ay talagang it will failed. 8,000 to 12,000 na ang namatay so wag na nating antayin yan sa inyong mga kabataan na dumating pa yan sino pa ang mga-ingay ngayon kung kayo pa ang nabura.

I: What is the role of your Party inside or outside of the Congress?

Cong. Zarate: Well ang pagkilos ng BAYANMUNA well sabi ko nga hindi lang sa loob ng kongreso. Dahil nga ang BAYANMUNA ay mga chapters yan sa buong bansa kabahagi ng kanyang trabaho ay pag-oorganisa ng mga miyembro ng chapters kapag nag-rely sakanila a pagpupukaw sa mas marami pang mamamayan. Kagaya ngayon may mga on going kaming meetings na pina-iintindi naming sakanila kung ano itong "TRAIN"or Tax Reform for Acceleration and Inclusion Bill na pinasa rin ng kongreso at nilabanan din namin initially kabahagi kami ng nagtutulak ng Tax Reform pero ang final output kasi na lumabas sa kongreso sa tingin naming magpapabigat sa mga mamamayan meron benepisyong ibinigay sa kaliwang kamay pero binawi naman ng kanang kamay dahil generally sa 2018 ipapasa din nating ang napa-karaming bagong tax at dahil itong mga tax na ito ay ipapasa naman ng mga kapitalista so actually tayo ang mahihirapan, so ayun yun sa labas ng kongreso maliban dun sa pagpupukaw, pagmomobilisa nakikipagunayan din kami sa iba pang mga organisasyon pa.

I: Aside from creating or proposing bills/ laws for the sector/s, what else are the other things that your Party is doing to help your constituents/ members to be more productive and well-function to our community?

Cong. Zarate: Well to be candid noong andyan pa ang PDA, hindi naman sa lahat ng panahon nabigyan kami ng PDAF panapanahon din syempre noong 2001 yan yung taon na pumasok sa kongreso si Arroyo dahil napatalsik si Estrada at early years there's have a distribution meron ding PDAF na na-punta sa BAYANMUNA, BAYANMUNA lang kasi ang party noon e wala munang ibang partylist noon but 2001 and I think by 2004 ng manawagan ang BAYANMUNA na mag-resign (Arroyo) dahil nga doon sa "Hello Garci"ang BAYANMUNA ay nanawagan na umalis at magresing si Arroyo dahil dun di na kami nabigyan ng PDAF. Ang PDAF ay part ng budget ni Arroyo yan so pwede nyang sabihin na "Bigyan yan, ito hindi"during that time ng may PDAF pa ang BAYANMUNA may mga programa kami like scholarships etc. siguro ang isa naming ipagmamalaki ay ni hindi kami ni isang beses nasangkot sa isang iskandalo dahil sa kahuli-hulihang centavo napunta yan sa mga proyek-to halimbawa ang BAYANMUNA may programang "Batang Mag-aaral"para yun sa pagpapa-aral sa mga estudyante "Bayang Malusog"reporma sa health at iba pang mga programa. Since ngayon hindi kami binigyan hindi pa rin kami papatibag panapanahon lang yan kagaya ngayon sa mga chapters naming they have their own programs para matulugan ang kanilang mga miyembro halimbawa ditto sa chapter sa Pangasinan, may mga fund raising sila and ang mga naiipon nila ay napupunta dun sa sa mga programa nila but then ang tingin naming ito ay mga panandaliang, mas long term mas strategic kung serbisyong pampubliko dapat nakatuon sa budget hindi muna kailangan pumunta kay congressman para humingi ng tulong para makapag-aral sa isang pampublikong paaralan so dapat yung pondo andoon na hindi mo na kailangan dumaan kay congressman para maging scholar, kung meron kang sakit wag ka na dumaan kay congressman, yan ang strategic naming laban na ilagay na sa budget kung may proyekto man kami wag ka na dumaan samin. Pumunta ka sa isang hospital may sapat na pondo doon, pumunta ka sa isang pampublikong paaralan may sapat na pondo doon at pumunta ka sa iba pang ahensya dahil nasasapat ang pondo doon.

I: Do you think your members/ constituents appreciate the efforts and presence of your Party? Do you have any data that will support your claim? Can we have a copy of it?

Cong. Zarate: Sa survey wala kami nyan dahil mahal kasi ang magpa-survey but ang gains naming siguro kung may pagtitiwala pa ba ang mamamayan samin ay the fact na nandito kami since 2001 at mas dumami ang MAKABAYAN kongresita dito sa loob kongreso noong 2001 ng tatakbo ang BAYANMUNA kasama ang MAKABAYAN ahh ngayon umabot na kami sa pito, isa sa BAYANMUNA , dalawa sa ACT TEACHERS, dalawa sa GABRIELA, isa sa KABATAAN, isa sa ANAKPAWIS. Ang potential na pagpaparami ay nandoon pa rin yun dahil lumalaki na rin ang pagboto sa progressive congress ang isa sigurong mga challenges and limitations isa nga sa mga sinabi ko dyan ang pag-pasok ng mga dinastiya na politiko sa partylist kasi napakamura na sakanila imagine kasi pag kontrolado mo ang isang district syempre mananalo ka dyan syempre mananalo din ang dala mong partylist halimbawa may mag- kapatid ditto eh yung isa congressman sa district yung isa naman congressman sa partylist so doble agad, gumastos lang sila ng isa pero ang kikitain nila ay doble kasi malaki na ang budget ngayon ng isang congressman kagaya ngayon ang sabi nila hundred million ang hidden pork so two hundred million na agad sila so ayun yung ano dyan may mga limitations pero naging unrelevance ba ng MAKABAYAN or ng BAYANMUNA ang diba hindi dahil ang isang partylist umabot na kami sa pito dahil sa dito kongreso hindi sa nagbubuhat ng bangko talagang kilala kami dito as a different block we are part of super majority but we are MAKABAYAN block that means we can assort our independence in some sort of issues, we can support the super majority but I don't know kung kailangan kami magiging part ng super majority pero hindi naming bibitawan yung basic principle na tanang tanang naming ng pumasok kami sa congress.

I: Are there any instances that your Party failed to do for at least once, your Party's functions most especially in proposing/ legislating certain laws in the Congress?

Cong. Zarate: Madami marami actually we can give a copy of that marami ito pero ilang daan ang umuusad dito sa ngayon halimbawa mamayang hapon buti na lang umuusad ngayon, meron kaming tinatawag na EVAC bill, evacuation bill matagal na naming pinapa-ukala yan na dapat magkaroon na tayo ng permanent evacuation for our people hindi kung kailang magkakaroon ng kalamidad atsaka magkaka-undagaga kung saan ba pupunta, nangyari samin yan kung kalian nangyari ang bagyon Pablo syempre malakas ang ulan lahat pumunta dun sa eskwelahan eh hindi alam na doon papunta ang landslide eh di ayun maraming namatay kaya pinapasa namin ngayon yan pero several times isa pang halimbawa na nire-refile namin is yung Bonifacio bill to declare as Andres Bonifacio as national hero noong 15th congress pa pero hindi parin yan umuusad, isa pa yung to remove the value added tax on power ayan yung ano ko eh kasi batayang serbsiyo to eh bat sasamahan mo pa ng vat. Ang dami ang daming bills every congress nire-refile yan pero hindi talaga pero kalakhan sabi ko nga ditto sa congress pag-interest yan ng mga panginoong may lupa lusot agad yan.

I: Why do you think you fail?

Cong. Zarate: Well kalakhan ang mayor na dahilan dyan as an institution napaka-konserbatibo ng kogreso dahil ayaw nila ng pagbabago mas lalo na ang malalalim na reporma kung meron man silang gusting isulong na batas ito yung mga batas na maisusulong ang kanilang mga interest halimbawa ano ba ang masama sa pagsulong nung itigil na ang contractualization sa mga manggagawa bakit hanggang ngayon hindi nagiging batas yan> ano ba ang masama halimbawa sa itaas ang sahod ng mga manggagawa maraming makikinabang dyan pero bakit ayaw nila? Dahil marami silang negosyo dahil tingin nila mababawasan ang kita nila dahil sila negosyante dito, ano ba ang masama kapag wag ipasa na gawing pribado ang mga pampublikong hospital kagaya ng orthopaedic dating pampublikong hospital yan pero ngayon ano na? pribado na at sinong may-ari nyan? Si Henry Sy kaya ayan yung pinaka-unang mayaman ditto sa ating bansa dahil ang utak nyan puro tubo lang.

I: What appropriate policy would you propose in order to achieve reform in our current Partylist System?

Cong. Zarate: Well ayun nga ng maalala ko noong 16th congress nirefile naming yung ano dapat talaga na bigyan ng pagtutuoon yung gusto ng konsitutsyon ang party list will serve the marginalized at kahit sabihin nating marginalized sector, nagsimula kasi ito nung dahil nga yung pinasang batas ng kongreso may sinabi kasi doon na may other organizations pero ng ininterpret ito ng supreme court sabi ng SC ay pwede kahit hindi marginalized sector kaya gusto naming i-ammend na ang party list system ay talagang limited talaga sya na ang magrerepresent sakanya ay talagang galling sa marginalized sector so ganun yung gusto naming amendments in fact gusto nga naming tanggalin yung limit na i-tally na lang sa tatlo pero up to now sinusulong namin yan dito sa kongreso the absence of that amendments of 7941 tuloy-tuloy itong nang-yayari sa party list lahat na pumapasok dito meron nga dito ang pangalan ng kanilang party list ay "Ang Mata"so anong ano yun? Ang ang constituent's nila yun? Sa susunod ba ka ang pumasok na dito ay ang "Ngipin ay Alagaan" mga dentista siguro. Sabihin naman ng mga sabungero na marginalized din sila na kawawa ang mga kristo ang tawag dyan sa mga humahawak ng mga manok so mag-o-organize din sila ang tawag dyan ay "Ang mga Sabungero" pwede mo bang pigilan yun? Kung walang strict guidelines kung walang pagtatangi susundin natin yung sinabi ng supreme court? Ang bawal lang ang mga ma-jority parties ang halimbawa nyan yung mga liberal party, PDP Laban, Uno, nagtatayo sila ng mga small parties para makasali sabi ng supreme court bawal ang majority parties pero pwede ang sectoral parties so pwede kong sabihin na "PDP Laban youth party list"so pwede yun dahil hindi ka naman major partylist. Sabi ni president digong kapag nagging parliamentary tanggalin itong party list system dahil nanggugulo lang mas lalo na yung MAKABAYAN block maiingay daw so kung matuloy man yan federal system na yan dapat magkaroon na pa ng mas maraming party list kahit sa mga maliliit na local, tignan mo sa local level sino ba nanalo dyan? Diba mga mayayayaman din si Mayor si tatay, si Vice-Mayor si Kuya, si Konsehal si nanay, oh diba family business na, ayan pa pala yang anti-dynasty law nasa 1987 constitution yan but it was only in the 16th congress na yung batas naming is dumating sa plenary we refiled that in 2001 yan anti-dynasty its only 2016 ng mapanalo naming yan sa committee level daming debate nyan ang sabi naming dapat dalawa lang ang naka-upo dyan so sa committee level pumayag na sila sa dalawa pero ng umabot na sa plenary hall gusto na nilang i-angat sa tatlo diyos ko ang sabi ko kung tatlo yan eh di dynasty na din yan pero ang sabi naman nila pwedeng tatlo pero hindi naman sabay-sabay pwede yung isang senador, isang mayor, isang congressman kaya hindi na din sya natuloy pero we are happy na din kasi kahit papano umabot naman sya sa plenary hall noong 16th congress, ang nakalagay sa 1987 constitution bawal ang dynasty ang problema lang is ang supreme court ang magde-define ng family dynasty yun lang ang problema ngayon dahil kung dapat na nakalagay sa constitution na bawal ang political dynasty na bawal ang ganito tapos na yun pero ang sabi nila hindi daw sila political dynasty binoto daw sila ng mamamayan.

I: We know that we have 4 inviolable parameters in electing Party list members: 2% threshold, three seat-limit chair, 20% allocation and proportional representation. If you have given a chance to amend or reform any of the 4 inviolable parameters, what would it be? Why?

Cong. Zarate: Di ko na maaala pero bigyan ko na lang kayo ng copy ng bill. Pero ang gusto talaga namin is mas maging makatotohanan yung representation ng marginalized sector at i-limit dun yung sector sa marginalized sector hindi na pwede na kung sino-sino na lang dahil lahat ng mayayaman pwede ng pumasok dyan at sabihin na marginalized sila, example sino bang mayayaman dyan ayoko ng magpangalan pero meron ditong party list na marcos loyalist paano mong masasabi na they are marginalized? Bakit mahihirap ba sila? Bakit sila marginalized? Dahil Marcos loyalist sila? Paano kapag may mga nagsabi na Aguinaldo loyalist sila? Na Bonifacio loyalist sila? What will happen to our partylist system? Naka-defined naman yan sa constitution ang problema lang dyan is may "others"para samin ang ibig sabihin nyang other sectors is other marginalized sector with the same category hindi naman kasi pwede yung mga milyonaryo na same nila ang workers, peasants, urban poor or women's. So kami bukas kami ng halimbawa ng Children's and Women's pwede sila magtayo ng party list nyan dahil talagang disadvantage ang Children's and Women's even the LGBTQ talaga naman isa din sila sa disadvatange may mga stereo typing, kunyari mga indigineous people ayan yung mga marginalized sector, yes merong mga mayayayaman na moro may mga mayayayaman naman na indigenous pero ayan yung mga tinatawag na marginalized. Kaya kung meron mang pagbabago dyan is yung 2% threshold binago na yan ng supreme court.

I: Do you have internal rules and regulations that should be followed by your Party members?

Cong. Zarate: Yes meron kaming party constitution in fact it is a basic before you can accept as a member of BAYANMUNA iba yung mga supporters pero kung member ng BAYANMUNA may mga pagdadaanan kang pag-aaral may mga orientation after that hindi kami humihinto after the orientation ah 24/7 and 365 andyan kami hindi kami yung party list na every election lang na sumusulpot sa communities so in the communities kasi karamihan sa aming mga chapters ay nasa communities ano yan talagang buhay ang BAYANMU-NA sa pagre-recruit sa pag-o-orrient.

I: Are you that type of leader who's very strict in implementing your Party's rules and regulations?

Cong. Zarate: Meron kasi kaming structure ang chairman naming si Congressman Neri during our last party congress so ang President naming si Ka Satur, Ako yung Executive Vice, so in term of discipline dumadaan kami sa under executive council like halimbawa may nagkakamali hindi naman basta basta sisipain yan dumadaan kami sa process but halimbawa dito sa office porket ako congressman hindi naman agad ako ang masusunod dito pinag-uusapan naming yan so kung ano ang ina-articulate ko is representing the party list so ayan ang pinagkaiba siguro namin yan sa iba.

I: What are the preparations that your Party is doing in proposing bills/ laws and how prepared is your Party for the possible outcomes whether it's negative or positive?

Cong. Zarate: Well itong karamihang panukalang batas naming ay hindi lang dumaan lang sa naisipan namin produkto ito ng konsultasyon sa iba't ibang sektor kahit yung mga proposals solutions so consultations with our barrios sectors halimbawa bakit kami nag-proposed ng genuine agrarian reform dahil ayun ang sabi ng mga magsasasaka na kailangan nila bakit halimbawa may panukala kaming "to upgrade the salary of the nurses"and "bakit kailangan tumaas ang sweldo ng manggagawa"dahil part ito ng consultative process. Minsan kasi kapag hindi dumaan sa konsultasyon litaw kasi, kung ano-ano na lang ang ipinapasa ditto sa kongreso halimbawa may isang panukala dito na buwisan daw ang asin, sino ang tatamaan nyan? Diba ang mahihirap. Sabi ko nga violation yan ng 11 commandments eh, ano ba ang 11 commandment? "does not tax salt because it is !.asin."So magkano daw ang buwis? So piso every milligram ng asin, kaya nung pina-ukala yan gumawa agad ako ng sample agad kung natuloy ang batas na yan na piso kada milligram itong ramen na to alam nyo ba kung ilan ang laman ng sodium content nito? It's 1,720 grams. So kung sabihin natin na kada piso magkano na agad ito? 1,720 na agad kahit sabihin na natin na tanggalin yung recommended daily allowance salt natin ganun pa rin nasa 1,520 pesos parin ang aabutin. Kaya nilabanan agad namin namin dahil dito palang patay na agad ang mahihirap dahil ito ang kanilang kadalasang kinakain tapos i-tax mo pa ng piso so balik tayo sa tanong, in process of filing a bill even the resolution dumadaan sa process even samin after ng consultation may dumadaan samin may mga pumunpunta dito from different sectors tapos we conduct consultation tapos may legislative staff kami na ginagraph tapos we connectively and pinag-uusapan before we file the bill or resolution.

I: How does your Party formulate the bills/ laws that will be proposed in the Congress? Did you just base it in your own perception or to the beneficiary constituents?

Cong. Zarate: Well ayun na ang explanation ko through consultation at yung mga beneficiaries halimbawa noong nagpanukala kami ng batas na "to stop privatization of public hospitals"ang ka-relate naming nun ay ang mga health workers hindi yung mga health hospital administration dahil gustong-gusto nila i-privatize pero sa mga ordinaryong workers ayaw nilang i-privatize so adter the consultation nagdraft kami ng bill na ito na ang kasunod narrative referral so may mga bills naman na madali lang pero sa mga bills naman na technical ang ginagawa naming kumukunsulta kami ng mga experts para makatulong sa pag- draft ng bill halimbawa yung "people's mining bill"may mga technical aspects dyan so we invited environmental specialist we invited mga scientist from UP halimbawa yung mga miyembro ng agham para tulungan kami mag-draft ng bill halimbawa sa SSS kailangan ng actuarial studies kung kakayanin ba ng pondo ng SSS na magdadag ng pension based on actual funds, hindi naman basta basta kung sino ang gumagawa nyan may mga experts actuarial studies talaga na kinikonsulta talaga namin yan, kasi you have to be ready eh kasi yunh bill mo halimbawa dumating yan sa committee level matatanong yan kung bakit mo ba ito tinutulak halimbawa itong nagpasa ng "asin bill"kung hindi nya inaral yan mapapahiya sya sa committee ang purpose nya it is a health bill kasi ang sabi nya marami na daw nagkakasakit sa bato kaya dapat tax-an pero kung health bill yan hindi dapat ang tax ang taasan dapat regulation pwede namang gumawa sya ng batas na itong mga gumagawa ng noodles ay dapat ang maximium ay ganito lang dapat ang miligram ng sodium paglumagpas ka po dyan you will be penalies, ang tatamaan sila hindi yung mga consumer dahil kung ang noodles ang tatax-an ang user ang tatamaan nyun eh hindi naman yung mga manufacturer kaya dapat talagang pag-aralan yung mga batas hindi naman naming sinasabi na wala kaming sablay may mga sablay sablay din namang nangyayari kaya pagdating committee level bukas naman kami sa mga adjustments dahil ang process of legislations alam mo naman yan dito ah ano rin yan eh its an art of compromises, you can comprised on preferal issues but not on principles and substance kaya halimbawa yung sa SSS bill balikan ko yan dahil isa yan sa talagang napakalaking tagumpay alam nyo bang 5,000 pesos ang initial budget namin dyan for proposals increase everymonth but eventually we agreed on a 2,000 pesos, eventually pumayag na rin kami sa 1,000 pesos noong 2017 and another 1,000 pesos for 2019 to be realistic para may makarating na tulong doon sa ating mga senior citizens

I: Do you receive any support coming from other Parties or other legislators about your proposed laws/ bills?

Cong. Zarate: Well unang-una saming sa MAKABAYAN block ang numbers namin dyan is BAYANMUNA, GABRIELA, ANAKPAWIS, ACT TEACH-ERS, and KABATAAN partylist bali kami ang nakaupo ngayon sa kongreso and meron din namang other parties na hindi naka-upo like PISTON and etc. but so far five kaming partylist na naka-upo at nagtutulungan kami dahil miyembro kami ng MAKABAYAN but yung ibang partylist naman dito kagaya nga ng SSS they are also supporting us not because that is popular but we explaining to them ang importance kung bakit kailangan makatangap ng dagdag pension ang mga senior citizens in fact talo nga kami roon e kasi kami yung nagsulong pero satingin nyo kung sino ang nakinabang noong botohan noong 2016? Yung Senior Citizen Partylist na hindi naman talaga kumilos dahil milyonaryo na yung nandyan, ngayon naka-upo sila noong 16th congress nag-away sila dahil hindi nila alam kung sino ang uupo sa two seats nominees nila kaya hindi sila naka-upo ngayon siguro naka-reserve sila kaya naka-upo sila last May lang pero hindi naman namin masisisi ang mga senior citizen dahil kapag botohan senior citizen partylist talaga ang bobotohin nila and we don't mind dahil sa kagalingan naman ng senior citizen yan, what im saying is isa yun sa mga panukalang batas namin na we gather support from different parties.

I: What do you think are the reasons why few members of the Congress support your proposed bills/ laws and why they did not?

Cong. Zarate: Well siguro nga nadaanan na din natin yan kanina sometimes may mga ibang bills na sinuportahan nila because its popular second because it also affect their constituents halimbawa itong proposals naming.. kasi itong General Appropriations Act is a law so batas yan eh pwede kang magpanukala ng amendment kaya ng nag-petisyon kami sinusuportahan ito ng mga kongresista na i-restore ang budget para sa mga public hospital because it is for their constituents but sometimes yung iba ayaw rin example yung mga landlords ayaw nilang suportahan yung Agrarian Reform Bills self explanatory it is against their self-interes, sa interest lang naman yan eh kaninong class interest ang isusulong ng batas. Sa amin kapag nagsusulong ng batas dapat sa interest ng mga uri ng mga mahihirap at ng mga marginalised at dahil interest ng mga uri ng mahihirap ng mga peasants, workers class ay opposed dun sa interest ng nga kapitalista ng mga malalaking kompanya mga Oligarchs syempre nagbabanggaan yan they are not supporting your bills but their are so called "Safe"bills or resolutions pwedeng magkatulungan dyan.

I: Are there any challenges or problems that your Party experienced? Can you elaborate these specific challenges?

Cong. Zarate: Siguro ang specific challenges now in a relation to the party list system is how to strengthen the law by amending it ayan yung specific challenges and to give meaning to the mandated of the constitution and objective why there's have a party list system in our consitution dahil ang tingin ng iba ditto ay unique dahil meron naman tayong presidential at ang party list system is for parliamentary government but since we adopted it ang gusto ng constitution dyan is to empower the marginalized sector even it is talkin about empower unfortunately under the existing law na bystandardized aught with the decision of the supreme court pa like the floodgate sa entry ng mga fake partylist fake in the sense na they are register but fake in the sense na they don't believe that they are representing the marginalized sector. Second siguro na challenge is specific how we relate to this administration we supported the admininistration of Duterte because of his long alliance with progressive congress with davao city in Mindanao region when he is still a mayor mataas ang kanyang pakikipagcommunicate sa left at in one year start this alliance with Duterte is being tested and now we are evaluating if there is still a basis in alliance with President Duterte even what happen last year.

I: What are the ways or steps you did to solve the challenges of your Party?

Cong. Zarate: Well para sa amin is there is always a challenges that has bee there in the past and up to now may mga variations lang, because for us our real challenges is kung paano naming mababago ang ating society, how this systemic society problem? For us tatlo yan eh foreign intervation, political and social economic, and feudal relations and the bureaucrat capitalism where the government used as a business ayan yung alam naming problema. As long as this problem is present I thing our society will be more irrelevant. Kung babalikan ko nga kanina ang pagbabago ay wala dito sa kongreso kung hindi nasa labas ng kongreso. Ang pagbabago mababago yan kapag ang instraktura ay pinagbagsak mo at yung din dapat ang gawin natin.

Cong. Tom Villarin of AKBAYAN Partylist

Cong. Villarin: Well AKBAYAN of the citizen's actions party, politically it's a multi sectoral organization it is by nature it's a political party because under our party list system representation its either a political party or a sectoral party that .. join in the party list system election.

Cong. Villarin: Yes, so to specific sectors we have members from the farmers sectors that why we imposed for the comprehensive agrarian reform program. Extension reform, we also have members from the labor sector, workers, we have unions, social ...membership from different unions, we also have members coming from women sector, we also have members from LGBT commu-nity, of course one of the biggest sectors are also the youth, the youth sector and we also have members coming from bangsamoro and from indigenous sector peoples.

Cong. Villarin: Well.. ang prior to my being elected sa AKBAYAN to be its representative I was with the NGO sector, I was with the farmers in Mindanao but prior to that I was also a student activist on my college days in 80's and I also was with the unions after I graduated from college, I work with labor organization.

Cong. Villarin: Well terms of priority of course among the sectors have priority legislative advocacies for the unions now yung mga labor sectors our priority is ending contractualization so that's why we have this bill that would eliminate the all forms of contractualization, for the farmer sector were still advocating for a continuation of the land redistribution program under CARPER so and for the LGBT and the main author of the Anti-discrimination bill, sexual orientation, gender identity, equality bill, sojili. 3rd in the house, for the other sector women, we still.. well AKBAYAN was instrumentally the passage of the RH law and the cheaper medicine act and the also lately we have this well for the Health sector the Anti-Hospital Deposit law which just signed by the President, now for the Youth our advocacy, one of the laws now is already passed was the free tuition for college education, so I was the .. the AKBAYAN bill was also the counterpart bill of Sen. Bam Aquino in the senate so while there were many Authors so yung AKBAYAN bill was the one and was instrumental sa pag pasa din ng Free Education for the Tertiary Education.

Cong. Villarin: So well ... From the start when AKBAYAN was founded in '98. I was one of the original founders, I was still working with the farmer sector so we parang in '98 because the trend there was really the critic that is our Political System wala nanag political party, so meron tayong mga personality based ng party na finance ng by.. by billionaires NPC by Danding Cojaunco, Ramon Ang, Nationalista Party by Villar, of course the Liberal Party is from the king sino yung mga oligarchs, so Akbayan was founded on the belief that it should be the sector that could really pushed for meaningful electoral and political reforms in our Country that was as early as '98.

Cong. Villarin: Yung Akbayan they won in the first partylist election in 1998. So yung unang partylist election was in 1998 and since then Akbayan was already represented in the congress tuloy tuloy yun. Our first representative was Chairperson Eta Rosales of the former Commission of Human Rights, so focused on the advocacy there is really on human rights so akbayan, since 1998 was really knows for its human rights advocacy.. then after chairperson Rosales, meron din from the academe si Mario aguha and also became our representative then after that third was Risa Hontiveros we have Cong. Walden Bello.. Prof. Walden Bello then we have Atty. Ibarra Gutierrez no, then.. after that ako na yung .. yung pumalit.

Cong. Villarin: Well yung akbayan .. one year before the election o more that a year before the election.. scheduled elections we already have our own party congress. So.. so deligates from Luzon, Visayas, Mindanao, NCR will gather and the deligates will elect, who.. who will be the person to represent the AKBAYAN in the Congress, so we have elected that..that person we have a list. It would be number 1, 2, 3, 4, 5 nominees so that will be submitted to COMELEC no, by the early as October , like next year October, that will be filling candidacy already so doon isa-submit yung list, then start of campaign febraury,.. tapos hanggang May, so when you garner atleast 2% of votes so you get a seat in the congress, we have 1 seat in the congress but we have also a seat sa senate so Sen. Risa Hontiveros.

Cong. Villarin: Well sa ngayon naman its really.. the AKBAYAN is focused sa legislation so that's why talagang tinutulak natin yung mga .. yung legislative agenda, so usually during the party congress.. doon sine-safe ang iyong priority agenda so base din yan sa anong priority ng isang sector so sa farmers, sec. union, so sa LGBT, sa women, sa Youth no, so doon naming tinatakda,.. thenafter that of course pagnakaupo na sa kongresso na.. syempre that's when the process of legislation comes into place so ang kuwan diyan is critical is you have to be also be very active sa.. so legislative work committees like ako ngayon I a member of atleast mga 8 committees, 7 or 8 committes but even if im not a member sa isang committee I also seat sa ibang committees so ang congress kasi natin.. When you file a bill you should defend that sa committee so mga committee hearing s na gagawin so yan yung process niyan. Well we have the minority so pito lang kami na .. whos really in the opposition.. so since last year mga .. really .. we have to fiscalized on the majority, kasi in a democracy naman.. you really have to have an opposition eh, not just to oppost and propose but really to fiscalized scrutimized the policy, the budget no, but even our role it opposition like halimbawa in AKBAYAN, we always succeeded in actinga bill so kahit nasa opposition its not a hindrance naman na kung baga wala kang maitulak na batas so.. so that's have been the trade mark of AKBAYAN.. so even in.. even in.. kasi naging part lang siya ng administration during P-NOY the rest puro opposition kami Ramos, Estrada, Gloria at ngayon nasa opposition kami but AKBAYAN has been very consistent yan yung principle at tsaka stand sa isip.

Cong. Villarin: Ah.. yun naman .. basically ang sa mga programs to be materialized sabi ko nga base yan sa mga sector, so we have to consult.. sa mga sectors, the blue collars, so regularly I have to talk with them, meet with them, non workers meron din kaming regular way of communicating tapos .. again pag meron silang mga gatherings, big gatherings dun nangyayare yung.. yung.. pag seset ng objective at tsaka assessment din dun kung nagawa ba or ano hindi pa nagawa.

Cong. Villarin: In terms of.. syempre yung human rights is broad yan no, from political social economic rights, ang sinasabi natin dito is... Okay we have legislation pero part din yan ng gawa na AKBAYAN provide oversite meaning "oh may batas na, yung batas ba ay ini-implement?"so sumasama sinasabi nating na oversite function ng congress, now .. with regards to.. kasi yun yung importante eh, yung batas na kailangan ma-implement so pag hindi na implement yung batas, una sabihin natin hindi klaro sa agency kung ano yung gagawin, o kaya yung agency .. like halimbawa yung Commission on Human Rights no, sabi natin ang focused lang nila ay masyadong political rights so sinasabi din natin na tinutulak din ng AKBAYAN na tutukan din yung mga ibang mga.. mga rights sa Economic so part of that again, pag file ng bill, resolutions na to provide the over site no, of course ganun din sa agrarian reform tinitignan naming na .. o annually ilan yung hectares na dini-distribute na nang DAR eh kung mabagal yung DAR syempre during budget hearing kine-question natin yun.. so yun yung.. law, pag may law dun oversite ang gagawin.

Cong. Villarin: Well as I have said AKBAYAN naman we have been consisted as a fiscalizer na sa.. sa administration of course status quo so ang nakilala talaga yung AKBAYAN really first and foremost na isa sa Human Rights Champion.. as a Human Right Champion .. bit bit din ng AKBAYAN yung interest ng mga basic sectors no, so napatunayan naman yan sa mga .. sa mga bills no, then of course outside congress ang AKBAYAN naman .. meron din tayong mga organizing sa mga basic sector pag.. halimbawa may mga issue ng katawalian .. no corruption so ang AKBAYAN handa na kaagad yan na mag punta sa kalya na kami ay lumalahok din sa mga protest against abuses of Government against corruption especially .. so.. so ang work talaga ng AKBAYAN is both in Congress and outside Congress.

Cong. Villarin: Yung .. well ang AKBAYAN basically ang priority program is really organizing so.. So.. Next is how do you organize members ang organizing ng AKBAYAN is..on the territorial level so we organize at the Barangay so sa Barangay mag sisimula yan sa ano interest nung community so bakit sila.. magiging AKBAYAN so it's either galling sila sa isang sector like farmer, kung farmers sila meron silang demand na mabigay sa kanila yung lupa, kung sa workers naman is increasing ng kanilang wages.. kung baga tapos yung maging regular sila unions naman ang inoorganize, sa youth naman sa Student Association sa mga school, kung out of school youth pwede yung approach naming ay cultural kasama sila sa mga cultural, now of course sa youth .. may .. may meron din program for scholarship kaya ang ginagaw naman natin diba nagpasa tayo ng batas na free tuition sa tertiary, so ibig sabihin hindi kana pipila sa .. kay Congressman o kaya kay Senador kasi ang Objective natin itong mga supposedly Government programs maalis yan sa top patronage.. halimbawa ako si Congressman eh syempre yung aking mga constituents pipila sa bahay ko o sa kaya sa office ko para manghingi ng indorsement, so kaya ayun, free tuition. Habol din natin ang universal access sa health diba, so .. ibig sabihin si Congressman mawawala na sa kanya yung discretion na .. diba.. mamimigay ako ng "eto yung card, yung health card mo, throught the effort of congressman that's patronage, so ang binebreak natin dito sa system is talagang mawala yung patronage sa ating political system through mga laws that are relevant and would give equal opportunity, equal access sa nakakaraming tao dun sa mga .. mga specific program and services.

Cong. Villarin: Yes, precisely because an gaming .. ang AKBAYAN naman ang .. ang efforts ng ilang nasa congress mga laws na in the first place ang nagtutulak ay mga sector so syempre like yung mga farmers.. merong.. meron kaming grupo yung.. pleasant cocos, kasama diyan task force palay, kasama yung grupo ng kaisahan, paano sumilaw yung mga nagmartsa noon from bukidnon papunta ng manila para lang i-demand, so ibig sabihin .. dahil galling sa kanila yun diba yung gusto ng batas.. ibig sabihin sila din yung nag bebenifit doon tapos yung .. well in terms naman sa work data ang.. ang kuwan talaga is having been re-elected every election that's the.. kung baga primary.. primary proof na.. na.. AKBAYAN they supported kasi hindi naman yung party list na diba wala kaming pera, yung iba alam naman natin may namimili ng boto, may mga.. an gating partylist ngayon ang daming partylist na biglaan nalang nagsusulpot, in-fact ngayon yung richest member ng house ay galling sa party list, One Pacman eh magkano asset niya? Billion diba, so sa mga partylist ngayon may mga millionaires na talaga na .. na alam naman natin ang election sa Philippines ano.. so .. so ang primary proof is basically for a political parties being re-elected every election ang AKBAYAN tapos.. so yan ang proof talaga for a support and now we have a senator so.. with 16 million votes so that's also proves na ang AKBAYAN ay supported ng tao.

Cong. Villarin: Well. .. theres.. oo.. siguro, hindi naman lahat talaga ng bills maitutulak so may mga bills din like.. ang pinaka-fraustration din naming nun in the past congress 16th congress we have this bill, bago pumutok yung PDAF scam, so we have this bill na i-limit yung discretionary powers ng president over the budget , so.. so .. tapos yung savings hindi automatic na ang president lang mag.. mag dedecide so.. kasi under our present set-up yung budget, yung national budget malaki ang discretion ng Presidente, so ayun

Up Hill climb yun, dahil habang tinutulak ng AKBAYAN doon syempre kung yung administration party ayaw nila yung ganun, bills that would limit the .. the broad powers of the president over the budget, so ayun yung isang major na nagging fraustration naming.. when it comes to legislation, second .. yung .. of course itong sa Agrarian Reform bills na... oh sige magpasa ng batas merong distribution pero madami dito mga land lord din so hinaharangan nila, tapos sasabihin nila, pwede ba exempted yung ganito, pwede.. so.. so merong .. kung baga you have to deal with ano mga.. oh sige we take this, yung iba ibibigay so yun yung sa legislation you have to parang compromise din same aspect, of course yung panukalang na Agrarian Reform libre ka nang mamahagi ng lupa eh an gating constitution nagsasabi na pag may taking away ng private property ikaw land lord may just compensation yun so hindi talaga pwedeng ..ah.. diba kunin mo yung lupa ng isang land lord tapos hindi mo siya bayaran, so yan yung mga ilang mga limitasyon.

Cong. Villarin: Well .. ang .. ang karamihan naman ang nasa house ngayon sa congress.. mga vested interest yan .. so ibig sabihin, pinaka maraming house members diba.. itong mga milyonaryo, nandyan ang mga land lord, nandyan yung mga .. lawyer ng mga big companies mga corporations, so.. yun yung kakaharapin mo , so ibig sabihin pag nag push ka ng batas that will be against their interest haharangin nila yun and they have the numbers in Congress HAHAHA! , so sa Kongreso botohan pag mas marami sila, talo tayo yan so yan yung mga pinaka major, pinaka major is the House of Congress is still full of vested interest.

Cong. Villarin: Well ang critical talaga niyan is of course AKBAYAN has to engage diba,.. ibig sabihin when we engage, okay we discussed halimbawa a legislative measure and he reason out the length .. itong sa ... Halimbawa anti-hospital deposit law so nag o-oppose yung mga hospital, dahil daw silay maluluge, eh sabi naming hindi naman kayo maluluge na.. you take in patience sa Emergency cases, bakit? Eh kung PhilHealth yung na emergency cases, pangalawa, there also safe guards na yung mga Hospitals na pwede nilang ma-reimburse din sa PhiliHealth yung mga costs .. yung mga ganun to reason out, sa agrarian reform, syempre .. oh sige, pwede bang sabihin nila wag biglaan? Steps yung.. steps.. incremental yung implementation kasi constitution mandate eh, so how do you implement, so yung mga ganun kasi ang legislation naman its not all black and white na.. na kung ano ang nakasulat yun na yun so .. you also have to consider yung mga ganung .. paraan its .. it's not really compromising yung principles but it's the art of negotiating, its negotiating what should be included.. what should be sabihin nating .. recommended sa end game, so ganun talaga yung legislation.

Cong. Villarin: As to preparation .. sabi ko nga kanina we have our party congress diba, one (1) year before the election dun sa party congress big gathering yan, so lahat represented so dun namin.. merong draft, general program of action, so meron din kaming .. sa general program of action I- adopt yun tapos meron ding discussion sa legislative agenda so ibigsabihin in the congress palang dun na naming idi-discuss at I-dentify ano yung priority okay so kung na identify nay un, so during the campaign .. pagnangangampanya kami so yan yung aming iha-highlight "AKBAYAN ay tumatakbo at ito ang kanyang gusto diba, ma-achieve pag siya'y maupo"hindi gaya sa ibang party diba na kung ano nalang pagandahan nalang .. sing and dance so AKBAYAN is very platfrom oriented so once nakaupo siya kailangan niyang gawin yung sinabi niya so.. itong sa reproductive health , anti-hospital deposit, free tuition at iba pang legislation so.. ang sinabi ko nga kanina sa preparations halimbawa pag nagcommittee hearing so sasabihin naming sa committee "pwede bang imbitahin yung mga ganitong farmer groups? Kung ang paguusapan sa committee ay... Agrarian reform"so magdadala kami ng mga farmers .. na mga spokesman na mag sasalita talaga sa committee so re- request natin sa committee yan na pagsalitain ang mga farmer group pag .. ngayon dito halimbawa sa Anti- discrimination bill so meron talagang.. inoorganize din naming yung mga advocates na makasali sa legislation so during the committee hearing tatanungin sila, " ano yung posisyon nyo?"so dun na i-incorporate yung ... Na mga ganung mga sector sa bill na yun.

Cong. Villarin: Siguro yung survey hindi na, we... We... Really have... Focus group discussion sa fgd .. meron kaming mga regional consultation .. kinoconduct.. tapos meron kaming mga sectoral caucus na tinatawag..Para dun sa mga preparations.

Cong. Villarin: Well for us hindi naman mahirap dahil ang mismong sector na yung gagawa sabi nila ito yung gusto namin .. so ang trabaho nalang halimbawa dito sa congress we just put it in to the form na necessary sa bill pero yung content yung laman eh..mga sector na kasi sila din naman ang nakakaalam anong gusto nila so yun.

Cong. Villarin: Yeah, in terms of legislation again its important na primary author ang AKBAYAN so ang ginagawa naminco-sponsor tawag diyan you get "Co–sponsor" of your bill... so of course AKBAYAN belonging to the minority automatic with six (6) other legislator kasi pito kami so yung anim mag co- sponsor tas meron ding mga supportive na mga district congressman na mag.. Mag coco-sponsor din so ang sopinakamaganda as.. kung baga if you get many co-sponsor sa bill then mas mataas yung chance na ma–approve siya.

Cong. Villarin: Well ang unang una like dahil .. ang karamahin naman ng laws or bills na finile ng AKBAYAN ay bills of national application kasi kung kaibahan sa district congressman , akong district karamihan ng mga bills ko .. oh itong school building na ito ipangalan ko sa lolo ko .. hahaha.. lolo inggo national highschool .. sopag district congressman karamihan ng mga bills niyan ay local application so ngayon dahil ang AKBAYAN ay nationwide naman so mga bills of national application so .. so ..marami ding sila. So yung mga ibang naming district congressman na malawak yung pananaw nakiki-ta nilang importante so mag susupport sila sa AKBAYAN yung mga hindi naman sumusuporta ito talaga yung identified naming kumukuntro sa amin ..halimbawa si Congressman Coangco hindi talaga susupporta sa amin yan na so.. so.. may mga .. may mga particular legislator from the start na hindi yan susupporta. Mga landlord's mga big landlords.

Cong. Villarin: Well ah.. basically ah.. yung ..promotion protection of human rights .. being a universal value and in terms of .. promotion of human rights it should be a reflected in the sectoral advocacy so .. so like.. okay the rights of farmers to have.. diba.. Who are tiling the lungs.. They have the rights to be se-cure in their .. in the farm land . ibig sabihin yung ownership sa kanilang lupa ay dapat sa kanila, yung mga informal settler families yung sinasasbi nating "Squatters"no so ang politically correct term is Informal Settler families no.. again the right to have an.. Dissent ah.. diba settlement at hindi sila pwedeng i-demolish o i-evict basta basta nalang without resettlement.. resettlement within the city. yung rights din nang sinasabi nating ... Of course the LGBT community that why we have this anti-discrimination bill. So .. so ibig sabihin human rights being the primary advocacy .. mag kakaroon yan ng hugis sa kanya kanyang sector yung trade union the rights to organize engage and negotiation so this are all belonging sa sinasabi nating mga .. universal human rights no.. so yun yung parang priority advocacy tsaka .. to promote human rights syempre it should also be reflected sa mga sector.

Cong. Villarin: Well.. as I have said.. yun nga .. dapat consultations, dapat .. involvement ng mga sectors sa mismong legislation kasi importante na yung mga talagang primary beneficiaries mga affected sectors kasama sila sa dun sa paglaban kasi mahirap na mag file kami ng bill dito eh wala naming sumusuporta so .. dapat kung baga active yung mga sector dun sa pagpapasa ng batas.

Cong. Villarin: Ah.. well we have a lot of parang legislative bills like one ngayon we have a bill that strengthening the functions on Commission on Human Rights no... Providing it with budget with increased budget .. then we're also looking at the Commission on Human rights having prosecutorial power spwede na siya mag file, mag sampa na nang kaso its not less recommendatory .. then .. other advocacies pa namin na yun nga sa mga sectors coconut levy trust fund bill, we have yung.. meron tayong sea farers no.. Magna carta for sea farers so.. pumasa na yan sa third reading .. itong In city near city on site development... In city near city on site resettlement .. so so pumasa na rin yan sa third reading yan .. So we .. we have a list of mga legislative agenda na pwedeng iprovide namin yan .so.. so yun yung amin sinasandalan prioritization.

Cong. Villarin: Well new bills na ngayon na kasi we have filed I think mga close two hundred bills na .. Then sa twelve bills.. Twelve bills are nasa.. well pumasa na yan sa second reading .. then may bills pa na referred already to that committee so siguro mga twenty bills na dinidiscuss sa committee.. then twenty to thirty up mga ganon.. I mean for committee, yung third reading naman dose for third reading.. second to third reading..mga bills discussed sa committee siguro mga thirty... Thirty plus. Tapos yung iba ni referred pa yan sa committee so ini-ischedule so minsan may time na sabay sabay yung.. diba alas Nueva sa umaga may dalawa akong bills eh isang committee so kelangan kong mag lagare, so ganun yung istatus.. so once the bill is filed referred sa committee halimbawa bill on workers labor committee bills sa informal settlers sa housing so yun naman so yun naman ang major committee yung Committee on human rights committee on housing and urban development, committee on agrarian reform, committee on labor, committee on fisheries and aquatic resource, committee on health, tapos.. local governments, committee on Local Governments. Although yung mga bills din kahit hindi ako member ng committee pwede akong sumali dun sa committee hearings. Usually ang.. sa house rules kasi pag nasa minority ka wala kang chair, ang nabibigyan lang ng committee chairmanship ay kung if you belong to the House Majority so ang kuwan lang talaga namin is membership pero.. so that's the rules ng house if you are with the majority bibigyan ka ng committee chair o vice chair.

Cong. Villarin: We ah.. we have .. bill na parang reforming the partylist law.. una ang gusto nating ifocus sa party list law ay dapat yung definition ng marginalize sector ay kung baga talaga siyang ma-implement kasi ngayon may mga supreme court rulings na parang sinasabi maski sino pwede nalang sumali, so kelangan magstretched yan with the marginalized no. marginalized.. Either you come from the marginalized sector or talagang you been advocating for a long time in service ng marginalized, tapos yung reform pa rin sa partylist system ang gusto nating ma-achieve is.. of course broader na political reform.. pwedeng 50% ng house should be partylist and 50% should be district representative yan yung mga major na policy change na gusto sana natin.

Cong. Villarin: Yung twenty percent dun sa constitutional limitation. So sabi ko nga kanina mas maganda kung hindi lang twenty percent kung pwede fifty percent. So the total house number .. fifty percent comes from the party list fifty percent come from district. While at the party may focus sila sa. .. I mean national. Pangalawa, dun sa two percent goal na .. of course in minimum threshold .. ibig sabihin na .. papasok ka no.. you can.. okay lang yun na may threshold, minimum threshold. Although ngayon yung supreme court ininterpret nila yan na .. may ranking system, kelangang i-fill up yung two percent pero maraming partylist hindi naka two percent sinasabi padin so kelangan reviewhin yan ginagawa ng COMELEC now on the.. in the practice sa ibang bansa bawal talaga yung .. yung limit. Kasi in a party list system of election we have to promote na... sana mag co-allies magsama sama, so pwede kasing isang party can garner more than three seats kung marami siyang constituents ngayong three seat lang sabihin ng iba, hindi mag hatihati nalang tayo para.. kasi kung maka-one seat ka kelangan mo lang ng 300,000 three hundred thousand, so.. eh samantalang dahil may three seat maski makakuha ka lang two million o hanggang three seat ka lang diba, eh kung mag hati hati ang two million mo na boto kung iisa isa ilan yun ? so kung baga anim tignan mo diba yung three hundred thousand 1 seat diba. Yun yung .. diba yun yung logic nun wag ka maglagay ng seat. So we want to abolish the three seat. tapos yung last.. yung proportionality naman, kasi yan that's one distinct factor for a partylist no okay lang yung.. then yung proportionality dahil .. again its constituency based no. may clear mandate the bigger your constituents the bigger parang.. in proportion yan yung seat mo dun sa ... So yung proportionality, yung threshold, importante yan. Of course yung hindi nabanggit diyan yung talangang from the marginalized and underrepresented no. importante din yan, kasama din yan.

Cong. Villarin: Well..As a political party, meron kaming consti and by-law... So meron kaming consti and by-laws. Ang Isang unique about AKBAYAN is sa aming by-laws nakalagay talaga na "in every.. in basic party unit is the chapter.."so..yung chapter ay nasa barangay, minimum of twelve members.. so pagdose na kasi sa isang barangay or halimbawa sa isang school Rizal Technological University minimum yan na may dose para ma-considered kayo na chapter.. tapos after the chapter sa isang lugar halimbawa isang legislative districts merong anim.. merong anim na chapters .. meron kayong parang section ang tawag namin. So 6 chapters will make up a section. So usually municipal level yung section, ngayon sa section naman .. pag may minimum na three section sa isang lugar o sa isang legislative district pwede na kayong maging division, so division. So Chapter, Section, division then meron kaming regional council ang regional council compose of all division in the region so kunyare NCR, Region 3 so..so.. After sa Regional Council meron na kaming national council, ang national council ay .. 7 per region representation. Now ang sectors meron ding membership sa national council so like Labor Sector so automatic meron silang pito, farmers and fisher folk pito, youth .. pito, so siguro may mga ilang sectors kami mga 10. So each sectors have na representation then... Party Representative, kasi ang Party Representative elected by the national congress no, so the Party Representative, President of the Party again at large elected sa congress. Yung chairperson, so ngayon ang chair naming si Senator Hontiveroz,.. Then the Secretary General. So ito yung mga ... 4 elected at large .. so president, chairperson, secretary general then the party representatives. So ang ..ang ginagawa naming anim yung ili-list. Kasi isusubmit sa COMELEC eh six names nalagay nay un in order of ranking 1, 2,3,4,5.. so ibig sabihin kung two seat yung AKBAYAN so yung number two nominee papasok siya kung maka-three seat edi .. so ngayon meron kang tatlong spare tire.. so kung halimbawa hindi magqualify yung tatlo so may papalit na .. so yun yung requirement din sa batas no... well again another requirement pala sa AKBAYAN is 1/3 atleast thirty percent.. atleast thirty percent of the members should be women no minimum of thirty percent so kung chapter kayo diba dose puro kayo lalaki hindi kayo ma-considered a chapter, atleast sa dose merong apat na babae isa yan, sa leadership sa national leadership tsaka sa mga division, section, diba .. tapos chapter 30% parin. So halimbawa sa .. halimbawa sa nominee so yung anim na nominee atleast 1/3 dun babae kadalasan naman ang nangyare tatlo babae nominee tatlo din lalake, so parang.. tas marami ding leaders ngayon sa AKBAYAN mga babae, yung aming chairperson si Risa, presidente naming si Macris ..babae. Secretary General si

Keith babae din. So .. yun yung isang requirements. Tapos ngayon sa membership halimbawa Chapter kayo merong dues.. diba so ang kinukuha namin is I think one peso or two pesos monthly .. so ang .. ang collection niyan dun sa chapter, kayo ang mag ki-keep nung inyong dues no, tapos pag magkaroon ng ... Merong national congress kelangan mag contribute, sa national congress para kung baga isama sama naman sa pagkakagastusan. Tapos of course sa by-laws naman namin may .. syempre dahil ang AKBAYAN is Human Rights may mga members kami dati na syempre hindi sila sangayon sa mga pagsupport sa human rights talagang matatanggal sila, may mga members din kami na .. nag violate yung.. yung karapatan ng mga kababaihan nag kwan ka ng sexist mark or pwede kang matangal sa party, so you have to live by the principles of AKBAYAN so ang ..ang kuwan lang naman .. sa .. yun basically may by-laws ang AKBAYAN may code of ethics .. At infact yung last order namin is may mga umalis nalang kapag masasakit yung violations.

Cong. Villarin: Well ah.. sa party naman .. basically in a democracy syempre meron yang opposing bills, may minority bills, majority bills sa party, there were times na.. like panahon ni PNOY, so ang.. ang debate sa loob ng AKBAYAN "patuloy ba tayong maging ka-alyado ni PNOY or dapat umalis"so for six years yan yung debate, so may mga members din na who really express their views na umalis na tayo kay PNOY sa alliance, like si ... Ang aming congressman noon si Walden Bello so nung natalo siya during the debate sabi niya "dahil natalo ako , so he resign as the representative dito sa .. so ganun naman yung sa AKBAYAN. So we encourage healthy debate with democracy .. as he reason out. After the debate syempre kung meron nang stand yung party everybody should support, hindi yung sabihin niya hindi ako yung kuwan dito yung konsensya ng partido, yung.. yung.. ganung challenge, but that's a.. Intrinsic in a democracy na meron talagang debate, mag away kayo. So yun yung I think one of the .. biggest challenges but again ang nireresolba namin yan through discussions and debate, and transparent, ibig sabihin hind yung mag uusap lang..tapos .. " ay ikaw tanggal kana"so talagang ...

Cong. Villarin: I think yung major sa AKBAYAN.. ang kanyang Advocacies mga .. importanteng nasa mass media o social media kaya for the party.. importante sa amin na the message should be always out sa media, we stand on this issues so that's why yung AKBAYAN .. regularly .. sa mga national issues our stand on the issue so so .. yun yung una. So pangalawa importante din that AKBAYAN we have a specific constituency so.. ina-update din namin like halimbawa yung mga workers, labor union so ito na yung inabot sa ating mga advocacies, issue, they were all well inform of our advocacies, tapos same din yung stand nila like sa Endo, pareha yung AKBAYAN tsaka yung mga unions sa stand sa ENDO, eto yung sinusuportahan, ganun din sa mga farmers, of course human rights the universal values indispensable yun para sa AKBAYAN hindi .. yung interpretation ng Human Rights, eh Human Rights nga ..sinasabi ni Duterte na pati criminal daw eh.. hindi. I mean human rights na .. focus sa political .. political, social, civic..pag inabuso tayo ng estado kelangan mo ng Commission on Human Rights.. pero halimbawa ang rights ng isang pulis nag violate eh estado ka eh, I mean you are a policeman you duty is to enforce the law, kung nabaril ka while .. nasa duty mo eh syempre yung trabaho na habulin yung nakabaril sa policeman, yung pumatay, DOJ yan. Dahil ang gagawin ng DOJ is prosecution, filan mo ng murder charges and homicide so .. so yun yung mga kuwan..may rights ba yung mga police? Of course may mga rights yung police niyan, pero in performance of his duty tapos namatay siya diba, eh syempre anong pwede ibigay mo dun is.. bigyan mo siya ng award ng recognition pero ang sinasabi ang nakapatay ng police , diba nakipagbatbatan sila kay maute, nakapaggyera sa... So yung mga sundalo syempre may human rights pero yung sundalo, kalaban naman nila terorista mga non-state actors, kasi may difference yan eh, state actors at non-state actors. Non-state actors mga terrorist syempre they are treated as plain criminals diba, so sampahan mo yan ng murder, sampahan mo yan ng .. so yan yung mga gusto mong habulin, so ginugulo lang ni duterte.. hindi human rights pati namatay na sundalo .. human rights ng mga masasapano.. of course may rights yung mga police nun .. pero yung nakalaban din nila nun pareha din silang armado.. of course kawawa lang dahil namatay.. so for AKBAYAN we have to very clear specific sa aming message were been in government , were been outside government.. in the administration AKBAYAN din ay has position not just oppose lang ng oppose but.. meron tayong pinopropose na mga batas.

Cong. Villarin: Well ah.. AKBAYAN believes in democracy... So when we say democracy ito yung pananaw na .. pluralist .. malawak na pananaw niya sa pagtingin sa lipunan .. so.. inclusive, ibig sabihin isang demokrasya na lahat ng pagkapantay pantay... ang AKBAYAN din naniniwala din kami sa tinatawag naming .. kung demokrasya yan participatory democracy.. so ibig sabihin inclusive detail .. gagawa ka ng mga batas na paano sila maging inclusive .. AKBAYAN also believes in participatory socialism na ang socialism na kinuha natin is yung tingin , pananaw ng taong bayan na.. basically yung access to ..

diba.. to government support services.. may access tayo sa .. sa ... Resources.. natural resources. So pagsinasabi nating may participatory socialism yung boses nung mamamayan ay kasama sa economic decision making ng ating bansa .. now ang kaibahan talaga ng AKBAYAN compared with other.. of course sa party-list meron naman talagang party list diba na pera lang, ... tas meron din dito party list.. makabayan block, yung makabayan.. for us na.. yung kanilang ideology na.. yung diba pipito sila pero iisa lang yung mga nagco-command niyan.. so democratic pluralist na may pananaw sa pagkapantay pantay and AKBAYAN for the past 19 years consistent talaga siya I think ang AKBAYAN lang ang one of the .. hanggang ngayon parang ito na ang pinakalongest na party list na sa.. sa.. history ng pilipinas were very consistent. Tapos nakita din naman yung AKBAYAN kasama ang AKBAYAN sa meron sa mga legislation, then politically .. the only.. well... of course... MAGDALO si Trillanes, pero as a political party the... not over the socialist, AKBAYAN has manage and get a seat sa senate, diba. So ang kaibahan ng AKBAYAN in terms sa kanyang Advocacy napapatunayan it can also covern.. then for AKBAYAN its.. kaibahan din naming sa ibang party list we have mga mayors, we have local government officials in AKBAYAN, then full pledge members, we have Mayors, we have.. a vice governor sa sibugay, mga councilors, city councilor, municipal councilors, then we have.. also allied ng mga district representatives ng AKBAYAN.

Cong. Sherwin Tugna of CIBAC Party-list (September 26, 2017)

I: Good afternoon Cong. Sherwin Tugna. What is the Political representation of your party? It is a sector or for multi sectoral system.

Cong. Tugna: You are correct Neil uhm... according to the decision of the Supreme Court uhm... PARTYLIST group are not merely limited to marginalized sectors uhm base on ruling of the Supreme Court there can be a sectoral or multi sectoral organization that can be a PARTYLIST organization here in congress so CITIZEN BATTLE AGAINST CORRUPTION is a isang organization compose of different individuals and have alot of members and whose common and united ------ and aspiration and our goal here in congress -- --- is to promote anti corruption and to promote good governance to the entire -- --- so CIBAC PARTYLIST is CITIZEN BATTLE AGAINST CORRUPTION falls under the category of uhm... Multi Sectoral Organization yeah. So yung specific is uhm... multi sectoral party po yung CIBAC.

I: Do you belong to the group that you represent, so parang pag sinabi po.. Para samin na CIBAC PARTYLIST is may kinalaman po siya sa corruption so may ano ba kayong experience na kaso na hinawakan na may kinalaman sa corruption as a lawyer po?

Cong. Tugna: Well uhm... nung ako ay abogado pa ng partidong YES kasi nag simula pa to nung panahon pa ng 1998 eh so ah yung time na bagong upo pa si president joseph estrada and siguro mga bata pa kayo nun lalo na yung mga estudyante natin sa RTU uhm.. Political Science kasi 1998 pa yan 1999, ilang taon na kayo nun? Uhm.... So yun nag file tayo ng kaso we joined in the mass protest action so uhm.... Yun yung nangyare nun alexis.

I: As you represent those sector, what is your priority?

Cong. Tugna: Well if you were - up you will check the legislative records uhm... Ang bills na pina file ng CIBAC ay puro anti - corruption uhm... Strengthening the Ombudsman and meron tayong bill that provides funds to whistle blowers yung mga nag kakanta ng mga... Those who are engaged corruption, witness protection program, aside from that strengthening the SANDIGAN BAYAN, so freedom of information Bill were citizen are allowed to access the Government transactions of public planning ---------------- 80% to 90% ng batas na pina file ng o Bills na pina file ng CIBAC dito sa Congress legislation ay puro anti- corruption.

I: When did you realize that you want to represent this kind of multi sectoral sector in Congress?

Cong. Tugna: Way back 2000 - 2009, I was already part of the PARTY although in a different capacity as lawyer so syempre lahat naman tayo uhm... Pinalaki na may takot kung baga meron tayong good morals, values so ang gusto natin tamaang mangyare so kung saan nakalaan ang pondo ng gobyerno dun dapat sya mailagay, mapunta para in doing so ah... Kung pondo yan para sa edukasyon magagamit ng kabataan, kung pondo para sa kalsada magagamit sa distribution ng mga produce or products of farm products, it can move people, so ibig sabihin basta lahat iyan mailagay sa tama mabilis ang progress natin sa nation.

I: What is first thing you do after your party allocate seats in the congress, and how do you feel about it? So base po sa research namin sir ito po yung last term nyo as a congressman.

Cong. Tugna: Ang unang unang gagawin mo dyan neil, titignan mo yung mga gusto sanang gawin last term eh kulang yung panahon syempre na ngangampanya din kayo dahil hindi ka naman pwedeng nandito lagi ,puro bills... Malamang. Talo ka sa halalan so lumalaban din kami, pumupunta kami sa mga Barangay so ang ginagawa namin unang una ni rereview namin yung uhm... Mga legislation na gusto naming ifile, nakikipag coordinates din kami sa mga anti-corruption groups, good governance groups and we also go to the mayors Brgy. Captains para malaman namin kung meron kaming feedback mechanism para malaman namin kung ano ang nang yayare on the ground. In doing so, after doing that alam namin yung problema sa baba para alam namin yung ipa file namin idadraft namin na bill.

I: How does your party works in the Congress. (outside)

Cong. Tugna: Well of course yun na nga yung sinasabi ko sayo alex na kami... You can be the best here always delivering bombastic privilege speech but it does not necessarily turn into votes kasi, take note ang dami namin dito na nag aagawan. Kami ng ------------ for us to be published on television so we go to different civil society organizations, talk to a mass of people like for example students and we talk about good governance. Uhm.. And it's benefits to our citizens and how progress will be achieved in a short period of time. If the ------- ----- as you represent the CIBAC party. Ah natural hindi, so syempre yan naman ang essence ng democracy lalo na kaso nasa political science kayo so hindi sya... Hindi sya smooth sailing dahil kung smooth sailing dictator ship na yan, so rough yan rough yan kaya nga may parliamentarian kaya nga parliament to eh debate, disagreement and we always agree to disagree. ------ Meron, meron!!! Yeah! Yeah! Kasi much related yan sa anti Corruption kasi in reality uhm... Ako!! I personally believe na 110 million Filipinos tayo ah kung hindi mo aayusin yung... Yung uhm... Economic states ng mga kabataan natin ngayon hindi sila makaka tapos, tapos during there education 4 years still in college and 4 years still in high school, hindi na sila naturuan ng tamang values uhm... Parang napaka hirap uhm... Maisaka tuparan yung ang mahirap magawa nung anti corruption kung yung mga next generation uupo sa mga private sector, public sector eh discord yung values, nila so we believe in education, right natin, education that teaches values, right and correct values.

I: Do you think your members/ constituents appreciate the efforts and presence of your Party? Do you have any data that will support your claim? Can we have a copy of it?

Cong. Tugna: I believe yes, most especially, lalo na ang mga kabataan natin we cannot under estimate them they are.... They are well, a turned to what happening in the country they are aware, they are intelligent so not only in terms of tangible na nakapag bigay kami ng scholarship, livelihood o nakapag pagawa kami ng isang magandang speech o nakapag pasa ng isang batas, just by merely speakingand they.... They felt that you are sincere with what you are saying that good enough by being a good example.... By walking the " talk.

I: Are there any instances that your Party failed to do for at least once, your Party's functions most especially in proposing/ legislating certain laws in the Congress? Why do you think you fail?
Cong. Tugna: Eh yung din nalang tayo sa nag fail dun sa sinasabi ko sayong hindi yan smooth sailing natural baka.... Baka yung iba may mga kaso, o ayaw nila yung batas na..... halimbawa FOI bubuklatin lahat ng kanilang ari arian, o di may opposition so yan ang isang rason kung bakit nag fefail. Part ng majority, yes kasi papaliwanag ko naman sayo kung bakit kami part ng majority kasi wala namang perpektong administrasyon, lahat yan kanyan kanyang priorities, kanya kanya ng mga programa. Ako!!! naniniwala ako, this just my personal belief having here in... Having been here in the congress, 7 years guys uhm..I've seen the Aquino administration, 6 years, I'am now seeing the Duterte administration the have different priorities, policies so mayroon siguro out on a scale from 1 to 10... 6 yung nagagawang mabuti ni President Duterte hangang 7 may 3 na parang hindi pa sumasang ayon, so you are part of the blue majority hindi dahil lahat nalang ng 10 program ay sinasang ayunan mo sinang ayunan mo yung 6 to 7 pero you continue to... Not to agree the other 3. Diba!!! Like for example yung mga ilang panukalang batas yan.
I: What are the preparations that your Party is doing in proposing bills/ laws and how prepared is your Party for the possible outcomes whether it's negative or positive?

Cong. Tugna: Well unang una yun na nga... Gagawa kami ng mga consultation on the ground, pangalawa sinisilip din namin yan, tinitignan namin sa senate kung meroon na bang mga pina file na bill na ganyan o kaya may ibang mga civil society organizations na tinatop kami kasi syempre nandito kami eh may mga ibang research group, hahanapin din namin yan " hoy may materials ba kayong ganito? " kukunin namin yan babasahin namin tapos tsaka kami mag dadraft ng bill. So parang... Parang ikaw din sa pag gawa ng thesis mo. Kasi ang prinsipyo wala namang mga bago unless imbentor tayo na bagong bago yung ginagawa natin o taga Philippine Science ka pero hindi eh ginagawa natin kumukuha tayo ng mga data, information pinag sama sama nati yun like a chef tapos gagawa tayo ng draft thats how it is parang kayo gumagawa ng thesis ganun din kami. Mahirap, syempre kasi marami kang kino consider eh, realistic yan eh!! Di naman sya yung parang.... Yes! Hindi.. Hindi naman sya parang ------- item na pina file mo na walang ----- eh. Oh yan na yung tinatawag na nag lolobby ka. Yung... Diba nakikita mo kaming umiikot, kumakamay pinapaliwanag mo yung eto yung gusto mong mangyare. Maganda yan, maganda yan para pag nag bobotohan may numero ka n. Parang classroom lang pagka tumakbo kang Presidente meron kanang Plataporma mo sinasala mo na. "Oh pag ako naging Presidente mag aouting kayo lagi... Sagot ko ah hindi na ako mag kukuha ng funds. Well syempre marami nang.. Yung values nila as they represent a group of people kasi yung iba district representative so ikaw taga saan kaba? (Mandaluyong) so Quenie Gonzalez yung naka dilaw na naka palda kanina oh hinahanap ko yundiba so kung sa kanya base rin sa kanyang mga constituents supportado nila tapos gusto din nila yung bill na yan.boboto sya in favor of that.

I: What are the steps your Party is taking to accomplish those advocacies you mentioned above?

Cong. Tugna: Research, talk to other civil society organizations that has the same interest and same advocacies

I: What is the status of your current bill? Are there any support coming from other legislators?

Cong. Tugna: Yung ibang mga nasa 2nd reading, 3rd reading..... Actually for me maayos naman... It's up to the people whether to vote for or not to vote for dun sa currently... Maayos... Maayos naman... Maayos.

I: What appropriate policy would you propose in order to achieve reform in our current Partylist System?

Cong. Tugna: Ako honestly uhm.. Kung ano yung nasa batas nasa constitution uhm.. As implemented by Republic Act 7941... As further explained and implemented by COMELEC Resolution as the Constitution body incharge of the election, i think it's good. I , mean a lot of people and saying me have to reform the PARTYLIST system but in reality the way to reform it is for people uhm.. To vote for whom they believe are performing much well and not to vote for those who are not performing well, so for me kasi nandyan, iba iba... Nandyan yung progressive groups! You know that alam mo yung progressive groups o katulad kami.. Good governance advocacy yung iba naman urban poor, farmers. Iba iba.... Yung iba naman allegedly mayayaman so kung hindi sila gusto ng tao wag nyo silang iboto, yung iba naman regionalism mga Ako Bicol, yung iba naman Ako Waray so ang point ko honestly at this point in time for me, it may have a few flaws but in general it's ok in fact yung PARTY-LIST dito, sila ang nag peperform, perfect attendance legislation yan.

I: Do you have internal rules and regulations that should be followed by your Party members? Are you that type of leader who's very strict in implementing your Party's rules and regulations?

Cong. Tugna: Eh natural basta dapat maging maayos ka at wag ka, mag nakaw mag... So halimbawa kung narinig nyong si atty. Sherwin tugna na involved sa anumalya at pag nanakaw eh may problema tayo kasi Anti- Corruption yun! Yun yung ni rerepresent mo. Yun yung unang unang requirements diba, nakakahiya yan. Head ako ng legal affairs committee ako ang abogado ng partido Hindi! hindi! Ang President namin si Senador Joel Villanueva

I: Are there any challenges or problems that your Party experienced?

Cong. Tugna: Well in reality katulad nyan legislation syempre mahirap gumawa ng ah Anti Corruption marami kang tatamaan... Dun lang sa city hall kung saan kayo nandun... Ohh o kaya kukuha kayo ng mga lisensya mahirap kasi.... Mahirap mag reform eh you will see that in real world when you work aside from that bina balance din yung time namin... Gusto man namin na marami kaming batas na magawa pero kailangan din namin na lumabas para kumuha ng boto, mangamay kasi dito ka sikat na sikat ka. Yun pala wala ka namang nadidirektahang tao so wala kang boto. Gumagawa ka ng machinery, so yan din yung mga hamon na hinahanap namin. Of course we may not to do it in 3 years uhm... 6 years but the change, i mean I'am talking to you... Young men you will form. Part of the working force of our society uhm.. The challenge to have. A better society that is responsive to there needs, social needs of the people.. You will and what if kids malnourished does not eat going around the streets no food, no clothes on their back during addiction. Lack of employment. Corrupt Government officials those who steal, instead of those funds being given to the people these aahh.. There are things does not help our country more forward so very relevant yung advocacy ng Anti Corruption, now, tommorow and in the future kasi it's human nature to some. I hope.... I hope not a lot human nature. I hope not a lot to be greedy.

I: Thank you po Sir!

Congressman Ron Salo of Kabayan Party list (November 22, 2017)

I: What is the Political Representation of your Party?

Cong. Salo: Yung Kabayan Party list is a multi (C sector party. We have members from youth; we have members from representing yung mga urban poor, the rural poor; we also have OFWs; we also have some professionals including teachers; we also have government workers; sea firers; we even have tricycle drivers, so basically it's a multi (C sector.

I: Do you belong to the group that you represent?

Cong. Salo: Professionals, yes but the same time a government worker because I used to.. I have been working with the government since I was a student as a law student here. I was once a member of a staff here in the congress so government.

I: as you represent this sector, what is your priority?

Cong. Salo: None, exactly. None, exactly the what specific area or sector should I prioritize it's really more of advocacies. Yung Kabayan party list over advocacies are some in what we call Kabayan plus 2 (Kabayan + 2). Kabayan + 2: first in kalusugan, pabahay, kabuhayan so that's why Kabayan plus 2, edukasyon and OFW. So basically, those particular advocacies of current party list cuts across all the sectors. Lahat naman sila nangangailangan ng kalusugan, mas maayos na calusugan, na pabahay, ng kabuhayan, education at OFW. So basically these are basic services which all of the sectors are actually in their need all.

I: When did you realize that you want to represent this kind of marginalized sector in the Congress? What is the first thing you do after your Party earned seat/s in the congress? And how do you feel about that?

Cong Salo: I had come with this particular... I am the founder of this particular party list, I put it up when in some time 2009, I was still in Malaca?ang. I was undersecretary then executive secretary under President Arroyo that time I hand the.. I was encourage to put up this party list after I represented the Philippine Government in Geneva on Migrant workers, so basically it arose from that idea for the protection of the OFW's but when I got back and hand that idea inspired and talked with some of my same minded groups or friends, they come up with more or less better we approach it on a multi (C sector rather than just with the OFWs in as much as they want to pursue as I mentioned a while ago. Those core advocacies of Kabayan Partly list which acts addresses all. The sectors of society then we ran in 2010 unfortunately we lost.. Okay.. then 2013 we did not, then 2016 we did and these, the reasons why we got two (2) seats. Of course, first is now the current spokesperson and second, we're working out for third to be proclaimed soonest so as a replacement of the first. What did we do immediately after the proclamation of course to gather stakeholders of course the .. our stakeholders of course the members. The officers and the members and.. and supporters in order for us to thresh out the proposed measures that we're going to file here in congress.

I: How does your party works in the Congress? What is the role of your Party inside and outside of the Congress?

Cong. Salo: Basically as a member of congress now because I'm representing Kabayan party list of course I am member of several committees there are around fourteen (14) committees and two (2) which I the vice chair. I have no chairmanship in as much as often times that particular chairmanship is given to second or more senior members. I am junior, very.. very junior in that sense, so but I have vice chairmanship is education and I is second is World development. That and also member of committee on rules. If you are member on committee on rules that's a part of what they called leadership committee ahh.. leadership function so I'm my official title is usually is called assistant majority leader as a member of committee of rules so inside congress I'm attending a lot of committee. Hearings, sessions, and meeting with people like your selves but basically this just one of those things but.. more or less meeting with various departments in the government and pursuing the advocacy by Kabayan party list that's inside. Outside, we usually.. we usually go to other places pursuing our projects because that's the advocacy part. Within congress basically its advocacy part the Kabayan + 2 that what we're pursuing outside what we do the projects. We have projects related to medical assistance but sometimes it's being done here also because the office they assist with the department so the staff members they are usually doing that. Education we also have its just not exactly, we don't call it so scholarship because it's not enough really just an educational assistance we have more than 2,500 Grantees, second medical assistance more than thousands din recipients, projects with respect to Tupad program, we called that Tupad program with Department of Labor and Employment, the temporary work for the ****** and the social workers we also have tie up with CHED its particular ah not CHED. CHED yun yung education assistance, we.. TESDA DSWD as we do count. Then of course some of the projects, projects from school buildings, roads so those are the things that we do outside, of course they just don't do it alone, can do it myself, so we have the Secretary General of course traveling all over as well representing Kabayan party list. Of course, members of the board were assisting me because of course my focus is discuss among us this, my power is to the advocacy part that's my goal but respect to the projects uhm that would be their role the secretary general and members of the board but of course the people will always look for the representatives so that's the hard part. Because yung during those times that you should be taking some rest. You just need to go because you're the one being requested.

I: Do you think your members/ constituents appreciate the efforts and presence of you party?

Cong. Salo: Of course.

I: May mga nag conduct po ba ng mga survey sa mga staff? Cong. Salo: No, hindi kami.. No we don't usually conduct, we have not done that yet but of course that would be a very good move on what we do usually is meeting with the board we have regular meetings at least a month sometimes twice sometimes even thrice so we have that of course the members of the board are supposed to, we talked to the members, number two (2) we also have the social media account were most of the members are encouraged to participate.

I: are there any instances that your party failed to do for atleast once, your Party's functions most especially in proposing/legislating certain laws in the congress? Why do you think you fail?

Cong. Salo: So far wala pa, wala pa naman uhm basically when it comes to our love advocacies if you will know, yung kalusugan were actually of the primary authors of the bill yung what we call universal health care. Kami yun of course Harry Roque also filled his own version but actually the version that he filled is the one was basically adopted by "committee"that's one of the primary advocacies of Kabayan party list the universal health care. The Philippine Mental Health Act., it was just passed on the other night, we're also one main the main author on that the RH Bill which being discussed now, I was also the primary author of that, the emergency medical services which I've been discussing all over. I have so many bills really to count cause I used to be the consultant of Department of Health and often times I also represented the country general forums outside country uhm health matters I.. a lawyer by profession but I was immerse with the Department of Health second, kalusugan, pabahay, with respect with pabahay our advocacy in Department of Housing and one of the main authors the insite onsite city resettlement and also one of the main authors of that particular bill. Kabuhayan so far, we have not filed a clear bill for anything about kabuhayan but basically it's really projects, the one that I mentioned to you a while ago, Tupad and the ******* actually we also have projects in ****** Muntinlupa for Kabayan party list lent certain amount of money for your Bigasan ng Bayan so that's part of kabuhayan part, then Education I don't know if you heard the 3C's Bill no not yet heard about since it's about transforming the vital of basic education fund what we called 3 R's to 3 C's from employability to employment so basically the advocacy of Kabayan party list for each and every one of us is to empowered so how do we say that the person is empowered. One of is able to have the 3 C's, one ****** the first is critical thinking, the 3 R's means reading, writing and arithmetic, okay but well to K (C 12 is about skills, but what we're trying to say is first develop the critical thinking, each person should know how the ability to think critically it is not less enough that your able to read, write, and count. All data as the moment of information that you need are just in your fingertips name any data that you want, just your fingertips, click it, google and download. Questions are we able to use the data for a betterment? Of course, the answer is no, why? Because people don't have to critical think doesn't mean is first, second, it's about craftsmanship it's about competency ****** or the skills but the skills that each person should have should be related to where he is coming from, we have so many resources in the Philippines so many ..... I'm from Pangasinan, it's a fishing also, all in the entire archipelago or archipelagic country seven thousand one hundred plus island where are (7,100) such resources which huge resources. Question, Did anybody teach us how to fish? See so what for? Everybody's working, look at this, everybody's studying for what? To work. Di ba tinuturuan tayo mag aral kayo para makapagtrabaho kayo and see each person the life expectancy of a person, of males, or expectancy the life expectancy of males is 65.3 at the age of sixty-five (65) pag nagretire ka malapit ka na matigok. Females seventy-one (71) so the average is sixty-five (65) point something is the life expectancy sa Philippines at the moment but what di been teaching us all along is just to work, where in fact we will live for sixty-five (65) years and we are not just supposed to do work, we're supposed to live, nakuha ninyo, naiintindihan yung mga work where I'm coming from? Ang itinuturo sa atin ng education natin na inculcate sa utak ng bawat sa atin nag aral ka kahit yung mga magulang natin because that's the mindset na naituro din sa kanila ng kanilang education mag aral ka para makapagtrabaho ka, mali, nag aaral tayo dapat para magamit natin magkaroon tayo ng critical thinking magkaroon tayo ng skills para kahit saan tayo nandoon pwede nating idevelop, pwede tayong mabuhay di ba, with all these resources that we have fishing why does nobody teach us how to fish? There's so many farm? Why does nobody teach us how to farm? And how to farm well, di ba and this is the advocacy of Kabayan party list and ang ituro din nating kung ano yung resources na meron siya pwedeng gamitin mali yung mindset all those times na ang tinuturo lang sa atin mag (C aral ka para makapagtrabaho ka, ang dapat na ituro sa atin, mag (C aral ka ng ma-igi para alam mo kung paano mo i-craft ang buhay mo, you want to be a doctor so be it, you want to be a lawyer, lawyer by profession so be it, you want to be a fisherman so be it, yumaman ka bilang fisherman, you want to be a farmer, yumaman ka bilang farmer, pero ang tinuturo sa atin ng educational system natin, hindi wala kang pera dyan eh, kaya pumunta ka ng Maynila magtrabaho't mag aral ka para makakuha ka ng trabaho mo, at anong trabaho? Sa pabrika? Masama ba yun? Hindi, pero may yumaman na ba bilang employee ng pabrika? Wala, see so this is we're from my perspective from the perspective Kabayan party list it's so busting powers and I'm trying to break the silos that they called ****** because of what I'm saying all profession is skill base, I'm a lawyer, that's a skill, it's a skill to talk to you it's a skill to argue with school. It's a skill to have analytical thinking, it's a skill for me to be able to read and write well, and to argue in the courts, and to have my client be acquitted. It's a skill, my wife is a doctor but a skill also, kasama ko siya mag aral, in my case nag aral pa ako sa London but that doesn't matter I cannot argue in the courts, tama? My wife is a doctor but that doesn't matter kahit saan siya grumadweyt, grumadweyt siya sa UP but that doesn't matter kung hindi naman niya magamot yung kanyang pasyente. Engineers, it doesn't matter saan ka grumadweyt o top ka ng board exam kung yung tinatayo mo di ba bumagsak. What does it mean? It's a skill. Architecture, all of maybe many professions all of this skill based but what skills on the rest of the population have? Those who are not members of the profession what skills do they have? None, di ba, that's why kailangan mo pang pumasok ng pabrika para magtrabaho ka at turuan ka kung paano mag fold ng papel, sana kung magfofold ka din naman ng papel dapat tinuruan ka na nung nag aaral ka, di ba, para pag pasok mo dun sa pabrika magaling ka mag fold, di ba, there's something wrong with education system, and the third is character we need mold each person's character so we develop the heart, you call that you develop the person, what we need our life skills, each Filipino should have the life skill life skill means the ability to live and the ability to decide, ability to be the person you want to be, .., so how does that work "Teacher a person, how to, don't give a person a fish, give him teach him how to fish, that's a skill in order for that person to fish not just one piece, but to be able to catch more fish one hundred pieces he needs critical thinking, ibig sabihin kapag lumabas siya di baa lam niya kung kung kalian siya lalabs, alam niya kung paano o ano ang gagamitin niya para makahuli di ba, hindi siya lalabas ng bagyo di ba, ano ang mangyayari sa kanya, hindi siya makakahuli nakakalagay pa siya sa alanganin. Hindi siya lalabas kapag malaki ang buwan dahil wala talaga siyang mahuhuli, di ba, what he need is critical thinking and in order to ensure that the way you fish is sustainable, and what you are doing something in legal that's character, so it's a totality, of course OFW kami rin yung Department of OFW or migrant officers kami rin yung isa sa mga pan-gunahing authors nun, balik tayo sa education, yung transnational education, ako lang rin yung nag file nung bill nay un, pasado na dito sa committee. Nag file si Sen. Escudero ng version exactly pattern after the bill that I filed. The concept of transnational education is to ensure that top universities outside the Philippines will be able to put up their branches or campuses here in the Philippines so that's what you called transnational education because basically the education in other country has a.. was have/still have to go outside in order to earn a degree at sometimes nagkakaroon ng walang masyadong competi-tion within, so we're limited with few universities we call it top universities the rest hindi nakaka, because there's not much competition they just they still meant come to go outside in order for them to be able to earn a degree, so ayun.

I: Do you receive any support coming from other parties or other legislators about your proposed laws/bills?

Cong. Salo: Yes, maraming nagco-co-author. Actually pinirmahan ko kanina, isa sa mga nagrerequest ng co-authorship.

I: What do you think are the reason why they support your proposed bills/ laws and why did not?

Cong. Salo: Basically yung mga pinopropose din ng bill ng Kabayan party list are really related dun sa mga advocacy nay un, on the same time mapapansin din ninyo there are something na just from taken from the meal, di ba ibig sabihin hindi lang kung ano yung nakahain na dyan, pumili kami kumuha kami at finile namin these are bill well thought out, pinagisipang maigi, tinasa, malalim na more effort for put it into it, that's why kung mapapansin ninyo often times kami lang yung may version nay un kami lang yung nagfafile na ganun, so basically yung iba ngayon nagcoco-author dun sa mas medaling ano sa student for discount we're the one, we want it to institutionalized kinopya rin niya wala pa naming ginagawa noon, ngayon ako na merong nag file noon, student for discount, institutionalization may mga ibang file nay un ngayon meron din kami nun, number two of course regular ng salaries ng mga barangay officials kasi honorary hanggang ngayon.

I: What do you think are the reason why they did not support your proposed bills/laws?

Cong. Salo: Basically hindi sa ayaw, I supposed really it's more of kasi hindi ko ma-experience na may mag ano but basically hindi naman kasi ako umiikot dyan para mag pa-co-author, I'm not that type na humihingi ng "Uy paki-author naman. Paki-co-author naman nito."I only uhm sign those matters pinapadala nila dito para mag co-author sasabihin nila sa akin "Uy, mag co-author kami ah", okay, but I don't unlike most people maiexperience mo siguro yun yung sinasabi mo "rejection"kung nagpapadala ako ng mga co-authorship forms sa kanila, in my case hindi eh, so I just, sila yung kusang nagpapadala ng gusting maki-co-author.

I: what appropriate policy would you propose in order to achieve reform in our current partylist system?

Cong. Salo: Kanina pinaguusapan naming yung proposed sa party list system dun sa Fidel form and I'm the one tasked of course and aim ng lahat is to ensure "legitimate"party list so it's a question of how to ensure that the party list will not "bastardized". Meaning legitimate groups or sectors are being represented.

I: meron po kasi kaming kopya ng 4 inviolable parameters ng partylist na dinefine ng court under veteran federation party in comelec, yung una po yung 20% allocation, then yung second po is 2% threshold, then yung pangat-lo po is yung the 3 seat limit rule, then yung pang apat po yung proportional representation, sa tingin niyo sir ano po doon yung dapat pong tanggalin or yung dapat parin pong istay sa reform ng partylist system?

Cong. Salo: Yung two percent (2%) tanggalin mo yung two percent (2%) kasi hindi na siya viable, that's the reason why kasi with two percent (2%) that the party list would be represented in congress is only fifty (50), you get mathe-matics right, di ba two percent (2%) times (x) fifty (50) that's one hundred percent (100%) di ba, sa ngayon there only there already sixty-eight (68) party list members here, so kapag two percent (2%) yung threshold na ginamit mo di ba, it doesn't make sense, sixty-eight (68) time (x) two (2) that's one hun-dred thirty-six (136) so beyond na that the reason why even the court itself even the Supreme Court cannot have difficulty reconciling that kasi under the constitution twenty percent (20%) dapat ang composition ng party list and that twenty percent (20%) pertain to sixty-eight (68) members kasi their three hundred ninety (390) plus members of the house di ba two hundred ninety (290) plus so twenty percent (20%) of that is sixty-eight (68), so kung sixty-eight (68) nga, kung gagamitin mo yung threshold na twenty percent (20%) ay twenty percent (20%) hindi siya, mali hindi siya lalabas that's the reason why tanggalin nay un, yung two percent (2%) threshold,

I: Do you have internal rules and regulations that should be followed by your party members?

Cong. Salo: Yes, of course.

I: Are you that type of leader who's very strict in implementing your Party's rule and regulations?

Cong. Salo: Partly yes and partly no. partly yes in those matters for me kasi may mga tinatawag na non-negotiables eh there's some principles na dapat lagging ano yuan but there are matters we called negotiables, so those matters na non-negotiables then I'm strict, with negotiable matters we go,

I: How do you give punishments to those who violates the rules and regula-tions of your Party?

Cong. Salo: Yes we have expelled a number; one of those is Harry Roque.

I: Do you give them such considerations if they violated any of your party's rule and regulations?

Cong. Salo: Yes, of course we exercise great attitude ibig sabihin in not much possible but dumadating yung point na mahirap, so in those instances then you meet the extreme measure

I: advocacies, functions and programs?

Cong. Salo: Basically we asked them to assist us, example on the medical assistance we also encourage them, it's not mandatory to them, we encourage them to assist example people outside them na alam nila kilala nila na nangangailangan then sinasabi namin huwag nang hintayin na sila yung lapitan kundi they should take the initiative in as much our party list anyway has the initiative working through that through acting.

I: Are there any challenges or problems that your Party experienced? Can you elaborate these specific Challenges?

Cong. Salo: The challenges really is with respect to Harry Rogue, that's the biggest challenges that we've been faced with, si Harry Rogue kasi, I don't know whether you have heard it actually he was my professor in UP College of Law, I was one of his favorite students, I was once his "friend"I became his co- faculty and became.. and he was one of our sponsor in the wedding, ninong naming sa kasal. That's the reason why nakapasok siya sa Kabayan party list to me because I'm the Founder Chairman, the founder of the party list. Nung pumasok siya of course.. people have that particular.. feeling, feeling of dominance feeling of.. feeling nila, feeling niya simply because I was once his student he treated me as if still his student, excuse me. So ayun yung nagkaroon ng concern, nagkaroon ng issue because he doesn't want to "listen" to even the members of the board.. sa kanya (C sa kanya lang but that doesn't.. that's not how party list works, in my case we always have a consulatation with the members of the organization so decision of party not decision of the person, thats what happened. So, of course the challenge there is nagkasuhan, nag file siya ng kaso, nag file ako ng kaso.

I: Do you think that your party's advocacies will help you to resolve the challenges that is happening in our society?

Cong. Salo: Yes of course, if you'll be able to understand well the concept of the 3 C's believe me this country will improve.

Congressman Antonio Tinio (ACT Teachers Partylist)

I: Good Afternoon, Cong. Antonio Tinio of ACT Teachers Partylist. For question no. 1, what is the Political Representation of ACT Teachers Party?

Cong. Tinio: "Well, Teachers, education sectors, employees, workers atsaka lahat ng mga interests sa edukasyon."

I: Do you belong to the Party you represent?

Cong. Tinio: "Yes.. Teacher ako! Ah.."

I: When did you realize that you want to represent this sector in the Congress?

Cong. Tinio: "Well, nag-decide kami nung 2009 na magbuo ng Party list para makalahok sa 2010 election."

I: What is the first thing you do after your Party earned seats in the Congress? And how do you feel about that?

Cong. Tinio: "Ah... well, syempre may mga finile tayo ng bills batay sa ah.. sa mga... pagkakaalam natin sa mga concerns ng sector. Kaski ano.. bago kasi tayo pumasok sa Kongreso, matagal na tayong ah.. nagtr-trabaho, aktibista sa sector ng edukasyon."

I: What is the role of your Party (inside and outside) of the Congress?

Cong. Tinio: "Well, inside, edi syempre pangunahin, ipagtanggol yung interest ng sector at maging mas malawak na mamamayan. Ah.. hindi lang yun teachers noh?... ah.. so ayun yung pangunahin. So nagpa.. nagpapanukala, nagpapasa ng mga batas, nakikilahok sa iba pang activities ah.. sa budget among others. Sa labas, ganun din ang advocacy. So nakikipag konsulta sa mga constituents natin sa mamamayan, active sa mga laban at campaign ano hoh. Nagra-rally, nakikipag-dialogo at iba pa."

I: What are the preparations that your Party is doing in proposing bills or law? "Nagco-conduct po ba kayo ng mga survey bago kayo mag-file ng bills or laws?"

Cong. Tinio: "Usually, consultations. So umiikot kami sa iba't ibang probinsya, sa iba't ibang bayan, nakikipag-meeting sa mga teachers, ah.. nire-report natin yung mga ginawa natin sa Kongreso at pinakikinggan natin sila."

I: Do you receive any support coming from other legislators about your proposed laws or bills?

Cong. Tinio: "Well yes, of course! Importante yan para makapagpasa ng batas, kailangan aprubahan yan ng.. ng buong Kongreso at least ng mayorya. So, importanteng bahagi yun, yung pagkuha ng suporta ng iba pang mga legislators."

I: "Ah.. Sir, ano po yung main ah.. ah.. main advocacy ng Party na ACT Teachers Party?

Cong. Tinio: "So Edukasyon. So karapatan, kagalingan ng mga guro, kawani ah.. karapatan sa edukasyon ng.. bawat Pilipino.. ah.. at ah.. yung ah.. pag laban para sa isang mas makatarungan, demokratiko at mapayapang at maunlad na bayan."

I: "What is the.. ano po yung pinaka-latest bill na finile niyo pos a Congress?"

Cong. Tinio: "Pinaka latest? Ah.. di ko na maalala eh.. kung ano ba yung pinaka latest.. ah.. kung sa sequence, ah.. check niyo na lang ah.. nakalista naman kasi di ko exactly ma-recall."

I: "Sir ah.. yung ah.. ACT Teachers Partylist po is a unified Partylist po, ano po yung position niyo? Kayo po ba ay Chairman? Or Chairperson? Or meron pa po kayo or meron pa pong other higher official?"

Cong. Tinio: "Ah.. meron anong.. merong.. so ah.. Chairperson ako tapos meron ibang officials yung Partylist."

I: "Ah.. next po, what appropriate policy would you propose in order to achieve reform in our current Party list System?

Cong. Tinio: "Ah.. well.. yung.. pagpapanatili na ano, yung ano.. yung Party list System ay para sa marginalized sectors sa ating lipunan, kasi nga ah.. nawala na yan.. ah.. sa pinaka huling Supreme Court ruling, binukas na practically sa lahat. Kaya nakikita natin ngayon yung mga Party list, ah.. kung susuriin niyo, yung mga traditional dynasties na din ang nabubuo at nakakaupo rin. So ayun yung kailangang baguhin."

I: "Ah.. Sir sa apat, ah meron po kasi kaming kopya ng four inviolable parameters ng Party list na dinefine po ng Veterans Federation Party vs ComElec po.. So, nandun po yung 20% threshold, ah.. 3-seat limit rule, then, 20% allocation tsaka proportional representation. Sa tingin niyo po Sir, ano po yung kailangan ma.. kung sa tingin niyo po lang pagna-amend yung Party list, ano po yung dapat mag stay or dapat na pong tanggalin?"

Cong. Tinio: "Una, hindi na yan yung latest ruling ng Supreme Court ah.. so ano yung dapat mabago jan? Ah.. well, katulad nga ng sinabi ko, yung pagtiyak na mananatili sa marginalized yung sistema ng Partylist ah.. tapos.. ah.. others, pwedeng baguhin yun noh? Para, halimbawa, tanggalin yung ah.. pwedeng tanggalin yung maximum of 3 seats para maging mas proportional ah.. kahit yung 2% threshold pwedeng you know? pwedeng mapag-usapan pa yan and so on. Pero yung pinaka basic sa akin is yung sa marginalized."

I: Are there any challenges or problems that your Party experienced?

Cong. Tinio: "Ah.. syempre, ang pinaka malaki palagi yung logistics kasi nga, nationwide ang campaign for Party list, ah.. grass root organization tayo so sa isang banda, ayun yung kalakasan natin na kahit limited lang yung financial resources, ah.. malaking bahagi ng campaign natin provided by volunteers noh.. both.. especially yung labor , yung kumbaga, yung actual na volunteer work noh? Kung ang ibang mga Party, kailangang magbayad, mag hire para sa pag-campaign, pagkabit ng mga posters, pag-ikot and etc. Tayo, largely volunteer yan. So malaking bagay yun. Pero gayunpaman syempre, kailangan mo pa ng pondo. So ayun palagi yung challenge."

I: Do you think that your Party's advocacy will help you to resolve the challenges that are happening in our society?

Cong. Tinio: "Yes of course! Dahil isa sa mga ah.. ah.. basic na karapatan ng mga Pilipino ay yung Edukasyon ah.. at karamihan ng mga Pilipino hindi naman ah.. sa totoo lang, halos malaking bahagi hindi nga nakakatapos kahit ng highschool, hindi nakakakumpleto ng highschool. So you know, hindi uunlad ang ating lipunan kung ah.. kahit yung access to complete basic education ay hindi man lang naga-garantiya.. lalo pa yung kolehiyo so kaya definitely, yung ating core advocacy ay mahalaga yan."

I: What makes your Party differ from other Partylist?

Cong. Tinio: "Ah.. Well.. well.. dun sa sector natin, edukasyon hindi naman lahat ganyan na.. pangalawa, ah.. kaming mga kinatawan ay mismong galing sa sector hindi tulad ng iba. Ah... tapos masasabi nating unlike other the majority of Partylist currently in Congress, eh.. ah.. talagang ah.. you know, ginagampanan natin yung papel bilang tagapagsalita para sa marginalized sectors. So ayun yung gagampanan natin."

I: "Sir, follow up question lang po, yung dun po sa functions niyo po, ng Party niyo, katanungan lang po na meron po ba kayong mga other ino-offer na programs like livelihood programs or scholarship grants?

Cong. Tinio: "Ah.. wala tayong ganyan pero dati, habang may sistema tayo ng PDAF, sa first term natin, meron tayong mga scholarships for teachers, mga nag M-MA, PhD, ganyan. Pero mula ng ma-abolished na yang PDAF at ang posisyon na natin is for the abolition of the pork barrel system, wala na tayong ganyan noh.. mga proyekto whether scholarship or yung mga building, infrastructure and so on. So talagang mula 2013 onwards at nare (Celect na tayo ay both in 2013 and then again in the 2016 elections, purely on advocacy, sa mga issues noh? Hindi tayo umaasa sa pork barrel at patunay na hindi kailangan ng pork barrel para makagampan bilang isang legislator."

I: "Sir, another po, yung dun po sa organizational paradigm niyo po, diba po nationwide po ang ACT Teachers, meron po ba kayo kada representatives, ano po yun? By district or by region na po yun yung mga reprsentatives niyo?"

Cong. Tinio: "Well, may mga chapters tayo throughout the country so yes, in every region, meron tayong matatagpuang mga organizations, members ng ACT Teachers."

Cong. Gary Alejano of MAGDALO Partylist (November 29, 2017)

I: Good day Sir!, We're from Rizal Technological University, 4th year students taking up Bachelor of Arts in Political Science and we're undertaking a thesis proposal entitled "Party list System: Its Advocacies, Functions and Program Involvement". So for question no.1 po, what is the Political Representation of your Party, the Magdalo Party?"

Cong. Alejano: Uhm as you may have heard from other party list repre-sentativesang party list kasi it's either political organization or uhm people's organization so .. sa Magdalo party list is a sectoral representation it is not a political party dito sa congress Akbayan is a political party uhm I think the Bayan Muna is a political party. Ang Magdalo party list is a sectoral party so ganunang category.

I: Do you belong to the Party you represent? The Magdalo Party, Sir?

Cong. Alejano: Well sige, so sectoral representation pag sinabi mong sectoral, anong sector yun or sectors that you represent. The Magdalo party list aims to represent the former and retired members of the Armed Forces of the Philippines and of course the urban poor and the youth so in a way multi (C sectoralsiya. But in reality not onky three (3) sectoral we will represent here in congress Magdalo party list is a multi (C sectoral representation and I belong I am former soldier member of the Armed Forces.

I: As you represent those sector what is your priority?"

Cong. Alejano: Ang priority natin kasi is security sector reform no.. alam niyo naman na nag rebelled ang Magdalo dahil sa mga problema sa loob ng organization and corruption as the whole so uhm.. even if the Armed Forces is not technically our constituents but they are the direct recipients of what every reform they wanted to pursue in a security sector like modernization of the Armed Forces ahh.. procurement law for the procurement of the pert of the modernization program, salaries, benefits, uhm.. yung welfare ngmgabeteranokasamayan oh.. so ang pinu-pursue natin meron tayong ahh.. major policy trust no.. good governance, anti (C corruptions, antidote to corruptions is a good governance and then ahh.. yung.. security sector reform pangalawayan and then yungahh sustainable development kasama yan sa sustainable development is yungahh.. pursue reforms on our instrumental laws, preservation of environment, reforestation kasamadoon and then ahh.. yung ahh.. of course security sector, beterano kasi ihihiwalay mo siya so representation din ng mga beterano.

I: When did you realized that you want to represent those kind of multi (C sectoral sector in the congress and what is the first thing you do after your party earned Magdalo seats in the congress and how do you feel about that?"

Cong. Alejano: Pang Miss Universe yan ha.. Ano ba ang aking ahh.. anong dumaan.. ano bang nararanasan ko bakit, ano bang na-realized ko bakit gusto kong mag join? Actually we are forced by the circumstances to join politics so nakulong kami. I was detained for seven (7) years no.. and because we wanted to influence policies in government that will benefit the Filipino people and primarily our sectors that we want to work itself so we decided to join politics no.. ahhyun nag confirm sa atin I myself I did not expect to be a congressman or representative this is duty, this is service no.. from a soldier this is a continuants of the service render to the country kaya I don't feel the ahh I don't feel the entitlement you embrace the entitlement as a congressman no..

ahh, ibayong-ibayong kultura dito. I don't want to embrace that kaya I feel nanaiiba kami dyan no.. so anoangginawa.. anoangginawawll natural, ahh.. nilatag naming yung aming legislative agenda, maliwanag dapat yon kasi the first time around we we're able to get two (2) seats, pangalawang term naito.. One (1) seat lang so nilatag na namin angaming agenda dinivide naming yung policy trust para may focus angaming mga representatives so si Congressman Acedillo yung isa dati so siya more on West Philippine Sea, Security Issues, I'm the internal security issues like Bang Sa Moro peace talks di ba so kaya yung may mga issue sa Mamasapano so dun kami heavily engage yan ahh.. nung nilatag naming yanuhm.. pero you should understand that the legislative process is a continues process no so may mga stages yan and.. before a proposed bill becomes a law it will go through the legislative bill papahabayan so while doing that so may advocacy activities karin like.. the issues.. important issues of the country.. ano ang ina-advocate natin diyan no ano ang stand natin at the same time we also take care of our constituents no by channeling the government progress of projects.. from the government to them those like scholarship, medical assistance, and we're continue to go around and organize the Samahang Magdalo so basically yun ang pinaka-major natin na issue.

I: What is the role of your Party inside and outside your Party?

Cong. Alejano: Well part list anoang role o ano yung mga activities? Well nabanggit ko rin kaninayan so.. dahil kami ni Gilmer is used to be from a soldier meant together in the marines no.. so.. so.. we engage heavily with Armed Forces, and the retired sector of Armed Forces.. kasi gusto nating-malamanyungmga issues inside the Armed Forces and then sa community work sa local government no, and since sa sustainable envoremont is part of our advocacies so we engage in so many activities like true planting, clean (C up drive. Hindi kami nagcoconnect sa mga politicians no because we believe that we should empower the people, kasipagsa politicians namanyun.. masyadong.. masyadong pulitika no so outside kasi ganito yan eh representation kasi is you we're represent the sentiment of the people kung ano man ang.. ang kanilang welfare yunang pinu-pursue mo so it's a representation but at the same time you have the responsibility to educate them because not all of the things thay know about.. issue of the country especially engage kami dito samga deliberation, hearings and it is also a responsibility to go them, report to them and educate them on what's happening in the country hindilangyung purely market driven kung ano yung narararamdaman ng mga taong bayan sige represent ko kayo not really market driven the fact that the.. electorates.. trusted your party list that means in a way they trust us to pursue something so pagkabalik sa kanila we tell them of what's happening in the country, educate them and the same time gather their sentiments and.. look out to their.. to their welfare.

I: Next naman po, do you think your members/ constituents appreciate the presence or efforts of your Party? And how did you know about that? Do you conduct any surveys or do you consult them personally?

Cong. Alejano: Sagutin ko diyan wala tayong survey tapos pangalawa pag dating sa kuntento ba sila o hindi, ganito lang yan even the President will.. the vast powers available to hil or to her would not be able to satisfy the demands of the people, tandaan niyo yan Presidente nayan nandiyan na lahat sa kanya much more sa amin na ang primary function naming is legislation it's not about execution, in fact that rule should be limited no kasi you are the ones executing policies and programs while just.. we just assist so ang nangyayari kasi ngayon parang nagiging executive ang legislative because may constituents sila to satisfy kasi kailangan nila sa boto di ba, pero in reality dapat mag focus lang kami sa legislation but nonetheless.. china-channel natin ito yung scholarship, medical assistance, support samgamahihirap, tulongsa DSWD.. mga tree planting programs.. meron naming from.. not fund coming from government from private sectors, scholarship grants, so merontayo nun ngayon, sabi ko nga kanina we can only do so much no and.. considering the nature of the organization of we are a volunteer organization and the concept of the Samahang Magdalo which the party list Magdalo party list use to be our constituents.. the.. they joined because they believe that they are part of the change we want to pursue, we are partners and the.. we we're.. we are telling them that.. they should not.. they should not join the organization because they wanted to get out.. or get something out of their organization they joined because they wanted to contribute their time and effort to the change that we wanted to happen in the country because the main purpose of organization is about responsible citizenship so ang sagot ng problema sa ating bansa ay hindi sa kanino man nasayo lahat so the change must start in you, so once that change.. happens in yourself you will be able to influence your family, you friends eventually your community so ganun ang pinaka-concept ng Magdalo, now kung hindi siya na-satisfy saamin.. dahil naghihintay lang sila ng anong makuha sa amin and then you are free to go out. Ganun lang kami hindi kami yung parang I will do everything to satisfy you. No! You have the responsibility do not pressure me to commit corruption in government just to satisfy you kasi yun ang nangyayari dahil gusto kong manalo i-satisfy kayo to the point nawala naming pera talaga ang opisinang congressman mangorap ako para ibibigay ko sa inyo the moment who will do that then stop this, ayaw na namin sapolitika.

I: Are there any instances that your Party fails to propose such bills/ laws and what do you think are the reasons why others don't support your proposed bills/ laws?

Cong. Alejano: Okay.. First.. dapat tignan natin yung legislative priority ng administrasyon di ba present administration. Pangalawa, legislative priority ng leadership ng congress di ba, pababa ka anong priority ng mga chairman ng mga committees na kung saan nag refer yung mga bills mo so may ganyan yun no, so pag ang chairman pa lang ay feel niya ay hindi o tama siya uhm.. wala nangyayari doon alikabukin ang bill mo di ba and then.. napakaraming bills no, and even if how good your bills are if it does.. if they are not in the priority of the leadership and the administration walang mangyayari. Now.. dito kasi walang maliwanag ako sabi kong dapat may guidelines talaga dito not only filing bills there must be a measurement as to.. whether you are.. masipag or not kasi dito mag absent ka hindi ka papasok wala naming problema eh, may sweldo ka pa rin, Congressman ka pa rin di ba, mag absent ka okay lang, ako I.. I make sure perfect ang attendance ko.. tsaka one of the most productive.. member of the Congress when it comes to bills.. filed and laws passed but the point is wala naming insentivesa akin anginsentiveko of course is we want to show to them na the Magdalo is doing his job kasi part ng advocacy naming yun eh and also.. kasi pagfa-file ng bills hindi lang yan just because you filed it, it's the expression of your desire to change a policy or influence a policy di ba so.. expression yan, eh gusto ko to. Ang tanong dyan mapu-pursue ba? Kasi colleague to, colleague so ganun ang nangyayari hindi naman yung nag fail siya.. kasi minsan may mga vested interest ang mga nandito ano ba yung policy na binibitbit no, alam niyo sa likod niyan may mga interest dyan, interest ng malalaking kompanya, political parties no, so nandun yun so kaya nga hindi pwede hiwalay ang taong bayan diyan, kung walang pressure ang taong bayan dito sa kongreso gagawin niya ang interest niya, ito this is a political house di ba may mga interest lahat yan tignan ninyo yung.. Microcosm yungpupuntaka dun sa isang lugar sila yung mga lords doon, pagdumating dito this is the "House of the Lords"di ba, kaya ang hirap mag adjust dito kasi.. walang direksyon, especially lang.. merong authoritarioan leadership dito sa house, it reflects to the nature of the administration..

I: How does your Party formulate the bills/ laws that will be proposed in the Congress and did you just based it in your perception or to the beneficiary constituents?

Cong. Alejano: Ganito yan sa.. along the.. in the process of.. productive consultation, kasi pumupunta umiikot kami ano nakukuha mo yun nakukuha mo yung mga issues na yun it may be personal to them parochial concerns pero collective yan malalaman mo rin.. pag nag consult kami pare-pareho so may concerns policy kasipag-usapan natin. So ayun so ibig sabihin dito nakatingin ka dapat example lang, example lang. "Paano na lang yung mga na-raid na mga adik", so that is emotional and specific no, i-angat mo doon ilan ba ang mga nare-raid na mga adik, ilan ba yung mga adik? And that is how you solve the.. policy problem.. gaano ba kalaki yan? Wide spread ba yan? Kailangan bang policy intervention? Kasi kung pupunta doon natural may nangyayari every day dyan di ba, so ang nangyayari kasi pini-personal nila labas and how can you react to that? When it comes to policy dapatumaangatka dun sa policy so as you consult nalalaman mo yung needs kahit may kailangan kayo kung hindi naman yun kailangan ng policy intervention wala yun kasi baka kailangan lang nila na maging maayos lang na pagi-implement ng mga programa so pagka-ganun, ibig sabihin pag dating ng mga budget deliberations or deliberations with the concern agencies pwede mong i-raise yun or we can raise that.. through resolutions or investigations or assessment para ma-adjust langyun.. yung.. programa o serbisyo pero kung meron talagang recurring problem hindi naaalis because of probitions of law doonkangayon mag po- propose ng bill to amend, to create a new law doon yun mangyayari so yun ang proseso kasi alam niyo naman hindi pa ganoong ka-politically mature ang Pilipino, magpakan.. ito sabihin ko sa inyo magpa-conduct ka dyan ng intellectual discussion mabo-bored yun.. ang hinihintay nila, "Ano ang makukuha naming dyan?"ganun yun mas interesado pa nga sila sa mga chismis eh di ba of course we cannot fault them but that's the reality so paano natin mababalangkas dito, doon sa policy trust natin no so makukuha natin yan sa consultation yes isa yan of course yung mga.. nanggaling din kami sa sector na yan ano bang aming grievances at that time when we went out and open stage na to against sa government so ganun ang process.

I: It is hard for your Party to formulate such laws/ bills to your constituents? Do you receive any support coming from other Parties or other legislators about your proposed laws/ bills?"

Cong. Alejano: Marami yan, marami, iba-iba yan,.. Maraming nag papa co-author sa akin no, kasi marami akong bills na pina file so gusto nila yon, kasi ganito yan mayrong original bill filed so nag papagawa ako, may researchers ako,... Pag pina file mo yan makita ng iba "gusto ko yan, papa co-author ako." Without me a single support, meron namang pag gawa ako ng bill, humihingi ako ng support, humingi ako ng support, merong mga 50,100 na gustong mag support, edi okay Ganda nun, so.... Not only that sa co- authorship but also sa committee, sa committee naman pwedeng humingi ka ng support sa chairman,sa mga members na.... Na maging present doon sa deliberation so ganon ang proseso nito hindi naman single lang.

I: Is there any pending bill your Party filed/ proposed in the Congress to support your Party's advocacies ?

Cong. Alejano: Marami!!! Actually I'm.... Siguro mga 2nd... In terms of bills filed in the PARTYLIST and 3rd in the Congress so..... Halos ganon karami... Mga na file natin na bills, so may pending? Yes!, marami yan, kung pending lang marami yan kasi bihira lang naman makapasa dito. Imaginin mo 294 kami dito so... Of course yung mga common nag bubudget, common lang yan, pero yung personal dito.... Like the.... Ano ba joint resolution para sa sweldo ng mga sweldo ng mga sundalo, yan yang mga hiningian natin ng support no,.... Additional na burial allowance sa mga biterano, yan napapasa na yan sa batas, so kung pending marami yan.

I: What is the status of your current bill? Are there any support coming from other legislators?

Cong. Alejano: Sabi ko nga, kung bills lang marami yan, eto nalang gawin natin,.. Pabigyan ko kayo ng listahan. Infact open yan sa website ng congress, tignan nyo lang don, yung finale... Open yan... Open documents so... Naka pending, yes! Una gusto natin na dun sa sector namin magkaroon ng increase sa combat pay, isa yon sa gusto natin na mag increase yung allowance or support sa mga beterano from 5,000 to 20,000 gusto nating mag patayo ng veterans medical center, hindi lang dito sa,... Meron tayong is lang eh, mga beterano dun sa Mindanao... So yun ang mga nasa sector na sinasabi natin right now sa iba namang mga issue.... Yung... Rural employment through DSWD, kahapon or isang araw pumasa na sa committee para support doon ss.... Sa mga walang trabaho sa rural, and then... Meron tayong... From technical working group it's a chair ipresent sa mother committee ang.... Reforestation requiring all of you graduating no, so irerequire kayo na pag nag graduate kayo so Elementary, High school, college mag tanim kayo so author ako nyan no... Bahagi ng ano natin yan so ang.... Pag eligate ng Criminology.... na hinahandle ng Board of examine lagi..iangat mo sa PRC kasi nga... Were worried about the... Quality of Policemen, lalo na sa mga Tokhang na ito ngayon, so iangat natin yan doon no, pang professionalism natin yan also authorized the.... The modernization and then... Reorganization of Philippine National Police no, dapat I reorganized yan... And ano pa ba... Ang isang proposal bill natin... Na magkaroon ng... Master development plan ang lahat ng LGU's required yun... Hindi pwedeng gawin nyo o hindi, okay lang, hindi... Irerequire kita, walang mga plano ang mga LGU kung saan sila maupo doon ako.. Kaya nga walang urban planning, yung mga bahay... Yung mga daan kalat kalat, diba.. Hindi ma connect, dapat kasi parang ano yan puzzle yan eh may mga plans lahat yan nakabuo ka ng Duterte, National Development plan diba, wala tayo non, kasi masyadong short term, masyado tayong temporary, Parochial kaya sabog sabog ang direction diba so.... Marami yan gusto mo ba tapusin ko? Eh kasi ano yan.. Nung ano.. I suggest tignan niyo nalang sa website.

I: What appropriate policy would you propose in order to achieve reform in our current Partylist System?"

Cong. Alejano: Actually in the last Congress...in the last Congress nag proposed tayo ng reform sa PARTYLIST hindi sya napasa as batas no,... Pero aside from the proportional representation pag sinabi mo kasing proportional representation.. Hindi yung.. Kokontesin, pareho lang tayo diba, pero okay lang naman yun pero ang reform talaga na dapat mangyare... Eh... Hindi langmakatotohanan ang representation, makatotohanan hindi naman yung... Eh hindi naman totally marginalized kasi hindi naman... Katulad niyan you represent professional sector, marginalized ba sila? Kasi pag tinignan mo ano ba ang marginalized diba, yung mga mahihirap mga nasa laylayan, diba.. Katulad niyan, they seek of a sector, hindi naman talaga marginalized, pero dapat makatotohanan ang representation, kasi maraming PARTYLIST dito extension of a Dynasty, Political Dynasty and mayayaman, , meron nga representation ng marginalized Pilipino, eh pero bilyonaryo... Eh.. Eh one (1) vote ka lang eh kung sa Pie nag aagawan kayo dyan kasi one vote lang sa PARTYLIST diba, buhusan ng pera ngayon din nag punta lahat sa kanya, nawalan yung mga legitimate... PARTYLIST katulad sa amin bumagsak kami nabawasan kami ng.... Kasi kami hindi kami nag.... May ibang PARTYLIST kasi traditional na campaigning talaga parang lokal... For example lang ah, ako congressman , o governor ang aking kapatid no, " Buo tayo ng PARTYLIST kasi ang boto ko ireplicate mo lang yan PARTYLIST na, para si ADING (kapatid) natin mag-ing congressman , edi congressman na kasi ni replicate nila yung boto eh, diba so ang.... Ang... Parang pag kampanya bara barangay din.. Hala!!! Namimigay din ng mga pera , nag bobotohan sila ng PARTYLIST, two (2) representatives na sila dito, anong gagawin nila dito? Diba, kaya nga makikita niyo yan by the way they participate, by the way they engaged... The legislative issues kasi ang iba dito extension lang talaga ng pamilya... Yun dapat ang reform na mangya-yare kasi although... Alam nyo ganito ah, napakarami nating batas para tayong nagawa ng batas.. May batas.. Tapal.. May batas tapal.. Eh magaling ang pinoy ikot ulet, diba. Kahit simple lang yung batas pag ang kultura ng pilipino naka ayos magagawa ang tama, eh sa COMELEC bayaran eh. Example gusto niyang ma accredits bayaran yung COMELEC accredited na siya kahit bogus, diba and alam mo yung hindi parin nawawala sa isipan natin na may cheating, diba ang electronic naging mabilis eh nag babayad doon , kung ilang seat ba ang kailangan mo o iipitin sila para na bigyan sila ng mga ganon, so ang reform natin is tunay na representation, tapos pangalawa hindi dapat sila gagamit ng... Pagkaka perahan ng COMELEC, kasi ang reform sa PARTYLIST hindi lang yan sa PARTYLIST eh may mga factor sa paligid kasi no..

I: We know that we have 4 inviolable parameters in electing Party list mem-bers: 2% threshold, three seat-limit chair, 20% allocation and proportional representation. If you have given a chance to amend or reform any of the 4 inviolable parameters, what would it be? Why?"

Cong. Alejano: Sa akin... 20 %, ako okay na yun no... Kasi magiging ... De-pletion sya eh, imaginin mo napakaraming partylist kasi sometimes... Ito Ni rerepresent natin ng district in a way , kasi multi sectoral ang district in a way nairerepresent narin sya example ang distrito ko heavy sa labor kasi nga industrial, in a way nakaka corp...Konsumo na rin ako ng issue ng labor di ba so in a way narerepresent na rin ****** 20%... will be enough ang 2% ang.. actually napakalaki na rin niyan ngayon sa botante.. ang threshold napakataas sa totoo lang kung maimplement that strictly iilan lang ang mananalo iilan lang ang mananalo kaya hindi rin siya nana.. implement ng strict kasi ang nangyari 2% of the votes.. 2% of the total votes casts to the party list so yun lang yun sana no pero you have to.. fill the.. seats so you have around 58 seats so pag napunan mo ang 30 meron ka pang naiwan na 28 so ihahati yan sa hindi umabot sa 2% from.. wala naman wala problema sa akin walang prob-lema sa akin ang proportional presentation yes I agree but the danger is pag hindi nareform yung true representation kakain yan ng mga bogus na party list uubusin nila yung seat yung mga tunay na representation na walang pera papatayin sa baba kaya nagkakaroon ng ambivalence ang mga miyembro dyan eh ito example lang One Pacman.. si Romero bilyonaryo ito na without offense to other party list "ang mata ay alagaan"di ba sabi ko nga magtayo rin "ang noo ay alagaan".. upaw party list.. so medyo kalokohan eh di ba.. ito without offense to Kabayan ang Kabayan out of nowhere yank ay Binay sinakyan ni Binay dahil tatakbo siya Harry Rogue sumama nanalo ang Kabayan 2 seats kaagad, well funded yan na-interview niyo si Ron Salo di ba without offense to Ron maayos naman yan pero ibig sabihin in reality of a.. the party list so.. well ano pa yung isa? 3 seats limit tama yun alam mo kung bakit? Kasi ano yan eh proportional representation di ba pag strictly yon imagine mo naman ubusin lang ng isang party list di ba.. kasi kahit.. ang gagawin na lang nila dyan kung napalaki sila ginawa ng Kabayan dati Bayan Muna lang yan Bayan Muna lang yan they have so many votes di bas a first elections in 1998 hindi sumali yan "Bakit naman ako sasali sa sistemang bulok"alam niyo naman siguro ang CPP (C NPANDF di ba, alam niyo ba yun? Bumabahagi ba kayo dun? Hindi naman nag oorganize ng mga estudyante yan sa mga ano.. so itong political side ay bahagi ng front ng legal front ng CPP (C NPANDF di ba so dito sila sa legislation marami ang.. malaki ang boto nila dati 1998 hindi sila sumali 2001 sumalis sila nag number 1 sila no ngayon saying ibang boto kaya nanganak nagkaroon ng Anak Pawis ng Gabriella nandoon yung Act Teachers si Tinio so nanganak siya ng marami oo so but they work together di bas a akin naman okay lang yan kasi in a way kita mo naman na masipag yung mga yan magan-da din naman na vo-voice yung mga.. mga issues ng sector.. mas okay ako doon no although ****** opposite end kami niyan mga kaibigan ko rin naman yan ang point natin ditto in the security.. ****** talagang that's a front eh na maliwanag na enemies of the states pero when it comes legislation and policy issues healthy yan kailangan may balance yun eh di ba so so far sa apat nay un wala akong problema doon kasi.. yun naman ang konsepto talaga ng party list no ****** problema.. dalawa lang sa akin ang problema eh true representation at tsaka sa COMELEC so ang COMELEC nga kasama sa reform doon.. hindi ko maalala lahat yung kasama sa discussion na dapat kapag ikaw ay naka-upo na yung next election ****** ****** yun hindi ka na dadaan sa proseso na parang nagsasubmit ka ulit kasi imagining mo naman meron kang seat tapos nadidisqualify ka di ba ibig sabihin on the first place kung di.. bago pa lang madisqualify iniipit na kami doon we are demonized before the public no we went through that rocess we went through a cleansing process nanalo si Senator Trillanes as Magdalo nanalo ang party list ****** Magdalo as a party list no so yun ang mga challenges pero gusto naming kasing umalis dun sa traditional no ayaw naming kumapit sa politiko ayaw naming yung pera pera.. nanalo kami pero challenge yan kasi hindi nga ganoon ka-mature ang mga electorates kasama mo ****** siya may tendency na gumanon so sa amin ang maliwanag na prinsipyo naming "we will not compromise ourselves just for the sake of winning"pag kami ay matalo kasi hindi kami naghanap at nagbigay ng pera so be it kasi kung kung baga ganito lang yan eh because we wanted to survive pero gumamit ka naman ng kalokohan wag na kasi ang sinasabi na "The end justify the means"di ba wag kayo maniwala doon because in the process yung means di ba it will define you pag narrating ka dun sa dulo sa end na sinasabi mo you are already compromise person so ngayon sa present congress ang challenge is of course.. we are in the opposition in fact ****** in the independent minority wala ako sa minority wala.. pure ****** no ayaw ko sumali dun sa.. challenge yan kasi lalabas ka dun sa traditional kasi minority ditto is also part of the majority parang kampihan yun eh di baa yaw ko sumali doon of course challenge na rin yan sa working ditto sa loob tapos pangalawa ang president mo ay hindi tumatanggap ng kritisismo isang diktador di ba so.. walang malayang discussion although ako I don't know kung nakikita niyo naman ako pag engage sa media objective tayo hindi tayo nagmumura hindi tayo.. so we.. we.. kasi ganito yan ang opposition pumupuna ng mga mali at kakulangan bakit kailangan yun para ma-pwersa ang administration to those fund to the ****** voices of the people ma-adjust yung programa polisiya at serbisyo hindi yung nagagalit ka kasi pag wala yan ditto na lang kahit mali yan wala kang trabaho so ang challenge.. iipitin ka ng administration.. kinasuhan ko ng impeachment bakit kasuhan mo culpable violation of the constitution talaga policy of killings pag sinabi mong wala akong.. hindi ako involve dyan sa killings sino ba binobola mo? Di ba okay sana kung wala tayong ears on the ground sa police sa military talagang policy ****** killing ganito yan ah hindi naman kelargang utusan kita na pumatay you are the president anything that goes out of your mouth forms part of the policy policy yan pag nagsalita ka in public kaya napakaingat dapat ang pangulo mag salita kahit yung mga gestures niyan maingat pag sinabing "patayin ko kayong lahat"can you explain that to all police men na biro lang yun? Di ba hindi naman magic or coinci-dence na ang daming namamatay sa kalsada pagkatapos niyang sinabi niya marami nang patayan that is a direct resolve di ba pagbenta sa atin sa China talagang treason culpable violation of the constitution shifting yes ating rights kasi right now wala na tayong activity sa West Philippine Sea isa pa yun sa aming adbokasiya an gating sovereignty and territorial integrity no so.. ang challenge kasi nga walang gusto na magsalita kasi nga pwede ka ipakulong kasuhan patayin nasa akin naman mo na kami hindi talaga qualified eh since nanalo na quinalify mo na kami tapos.. nanalo nan a-disqualify ka ano yon ibig sabihin non nagpapabayad ako.. bayaran niyo ako para mabalik kayo diyan nagiging source ng corruption so pagnahalo ka na ministerial na lang yon tuloy tuloy na so dapat bago pumasok higpitan natin. .

I: Do you have internal rules and regulations that should be followed by your Party members? Are you that type of leader who's very strict in implementing your Party's rules and regulations?"

Cong. Alejano: Tingin niyo strikto ako? ****** executive committee ng Magdalo pero sundalo dati so we are in a structures organization.. sa Magdalo party list we have the management so sa amin.. pag sinabi mong strikto strikto sa level ng party list pero you cannot do that sa constituents.. kasi sa constituents boluntaryo nga eh so boluntaryo strikto kami doon sa code because we wanted to embrace the code.. pag taliwas ka doon tatanggaling ka naming talaga katulad niyan.. alam mob a yung isa sa code namingpag nilahok ako sa election hindi ko ipagbibili ang boto diyan violation no so.. core values like loyalty bat ka sa amin sumasama tinitira mo rin naman kami at tsaka mga officers so tanggalin naming yun so ibig sabihin ganun yung mga proseso pag nag violate ka dun sa by (C laws ng party list you will go to deliberation pag talagang ****** to tatanggalin naming pag wala ****** naming pero dito sa taas sa amin sa leadershio talagang may mga targets kami talaga na sinusundan.

I: Are there any challenges or problems that your Party experienced?

Cong.Alejano: Dun muna tayo unnang una panahon ni Gloria panahon na kay Gloria.. nag file kami ng accreditation as party list hindi kami inapprove nung una kasi nga tingin sa amin kalaban ****** nasa kulungan kami di ba.. sabi nila they.. we will just use this opportunity to ****** blind followers and destabilized and tackle the government when you apply for accreditation to COMELEC you are joining the main stream you are aligning yourself to be part of the system bat mo kami pipigilan? You're pushing us away from the main stream kaya nga tinanggal ****** yung ****** law because we want the communist to join in the discussion manalo kami o hindi kung sa aming pagtayo ay sabi ng taong bayan "we love tatay Digong"di ba eh ang tingin mali kayo so be it di ba bat mo kami katakutin wag mong kontrahin yan hindi ka mananalo sa ****** edi wag di ba ganun kami kaya nga wala kaming pakialam kung.. unang una hanggang ngayon hindi pa kami kinakasuhan kasi nga hindi naman kami nangongorap sa gobyerno kasi kung corrupt kami matagal na kaming kinakasuhan di ba matagal na nilang kinuhukay kami wala silang Makita kaya wala kaming pakialam kasi wala kaming kinakatakutan.